A-AR

Comptroller of the Currency
Administrator of National Banks

Accounts Receivable and Inventory Financing

Comptroller's Handbook

March 2000

A

Assets

Accounts Receivable and Inventory Financing

Table of Contents

Accounts Receivable and Inventory Financing

Introduction

This booklet describes the fundamentals of accounts receivable and inventory financing (ARIF). The booklet summarizes ARIF risks and discusses how a bank can prudently manage these risks. One of a series of specialized lending booklets of the *Comptroller's Handbook*, "Accounts Receivable and Inventory Financing" supplements the general guidance in the "Loan Portfolio Management" and "Commercial Lending" booklets.

Overview

ARIF is the most fundamental form of "collateral-based" commercial lending. It combines elements of secured lending and short-term business loans. In its purest form, commercial borrowers use the value of their receivables and inventory (working assets) as collateral to secure financing to produce and market their products and services. The financing is then repaid by converting the inventory to cash, either directly or through the collection of an accounts receivable invoice. Depending on the risk profile of the borrower, lenders exercise varying degrees of control over collateral to manage the credit risk in the transaction.

Over time many variations of ARIF have developed. The collateral base may now include assets other than receivables and inventory, controls over collateral have been modified, and repayment sources have been expanded beyond the conversion of working assets. In addition to providing funds to finance inventory, ARIF loans are used to finance acquisitions, to restructure debt, and to tide companies through periods of distress. Manufacturers, wholesalers, distributors, retailers, importers and service organizations all use ARIF to meet their business needs. Although ARIF has undergone change, it remains essentially a means for borrowers to leverage assets to obtain financing.

As the structure of ARIF loans has been modified, the availability of ARIF has also expanded. Once the province of a small group of specialized lenders, ARIF is now offered by most large and mid-sized banks and many community banks. Borrower demand for more credit availability and banks seeking opportunities to expand their loan portfolios have spurred this growth. However, as discussed below, this type of specialized lending carries with it a higher degree of risk than most other types of commercial lending. As a result,

ARIF loans require more intensive controls and supervision. ARIF has several unique features. Most particularly, the source of repayment of these loans is dedicated cash flows from the conversion of working assets, unlike most commercial loans where the source repayment is cash flow from operations. (For a more compete discussion of cash flows, see the section below on "Assessing the Borrower's Operating Cycle.") The controls applied to collateral and cash receipts also differentiate ARIF loans from other types of commercial loans.

Most ARIF relationships exhibit **moderate to high risk.** Borrowers typically turn to ARIF when they cannot obtain other types of financing. ARIF borrowers may not be as strong financially as other commercial borrowers, they may operate in industries with high volatility or significant seasonality, or they may be experiencing rapid growth. These borrowers exhibit higher risk of default characteristics such as:

- High leverage.

- Erratic or marginal profitability.

- Limited working capital and cash reserves.

- Constantly changing collateral pools whose value can fall quickly.

Properly structured ARIF transactions mitigate the risk of default by imposing controls on collateral and cash. When an ARIF loan is properly margined and the bank applies prudent monitoring and control processes, the risk of loss actually can be less than for other types of commercial lending. The key is in exercising the degree of control necessary to manage and mitigate the risks — the higher the risk, the greater the control needed. To achieve control, lenders need significant management expertise, a thorough understanding of the borrower's business, good reporting systems, and ongoing supervision of the collateral and the relationship.

Because of the higher intrinsic default risk in ARIF loans, ARIF units often report higher levels of adversely rated loans than other commercial lending units. This is expected. By the same token, the collateral support and administrative controls used to manage these loans, particularly in well-managed ABL units, often results in lower losses. The lower loss experience should be reflected in the allowance provision and in capital allocations in internal risk models.

Risks of Accounts Receivable and Inventory Financing

From a supervisory perspective, risk is the potential that events, expected or unanticipated, may have an adverse impact on a bank's capital or earnings. The OCC has identified nine categories of risk for bank supervision purposes: credit, interest rate, liquidity, price, foreign currency translation, transaction, compliance, strategic, and reputation. While ARIF has all these risks, this booklet will focus on credit, transaction, and compliance risk. For a complete discussion of the other risks, refer to the "Loan Portfolio Management" booklet and the *Comptroller's Handbook for National Bank Examiners.*

Credit Risk

Credit risk is the current and prospective risk to earnings or capital arising from an obligor's failure to meet the terms of any contract with the bank or otherwise to perform as agreed. Credit risk arises any time bank funds are extended, committed, invested, or otherwise exposed through actual or implied contractual agreements, whether reflected on or off the balance sheet.

Like other types of commercial lending, ARIF's most significant risk is credit risk. ARIF borrowers typically exhibit higher default risk than other commercial borrowers. Credit risk is present in every part of the lending cycle — initial credit evaluation, underwriting, loan approval, loan administration, and, if necessary, debt liquidation.

Transaction Risk

Transaction risk is the current and prospective risk to earnings and capital arising from fraud, error, and the inability to deliver products or services, maintain a competitive position, and manage information. ARIF has elevated transaction risk because of the complexity of the products and the internal control environment. The risk encompasses product development and delivery, transaction processing, systems development, computing systems, employee integrity, and operating processes. Transaction risk can also develop when management or staff does not provide sufficient oversight.

Transaction risk in accounts receivable and inventory financing is primarily posed by:

- Internal operations of the lending department, including the need to properly perfect liens under the Uniform Commercial Code (UCC).

- Internal operations of the borrower.

- The potential for fraud on the part of the borrower.

- The failure to properly oversee ARIF computer software products offered by third-party vendors, if applicable.

Compliance Risk

Compliance risk is the risk to earnings or capital arising from violations of or nonconformance with laws, rules, regulations, prescribed practices, or ethical standards. Compliance risk also arises in situations where the laws or rules governing certain bank products or the activities of the bank's clients may be ambiguous or untested. Because ARIF departments exert a significant amount of control over the borrower's working assets, this type of lending can be more vulnerable to compliance risk. This booklet discusses compliance risk posed by:

- Noncompliance with federal and state laws, rules, and regulations. For example, a borrower may suffer financial setbacks if it violates or fails to conform to laws governing environmental contamination, health, safety, or fair labor.

- Litigation and other legal remedies (for example, lender liability actions) that may arise when the lender seeks to have a debt liquidated.

Credit Risk Rating Considerations

Considerable debate has surrounded the issue of whether the uniform inter-agency classification guidelines are appropriate for rating ARIF loans. OCC policy is to apply the uniform interagency rating definitions, as contained in the "Classification of Credits" section of the *Comptroller's Handbook*. These definitions take into account **both** risk of default and risk of loss in the event of default. Risk of default is generally a matter of the financial strength of the borrower, while risk of loss upon default is generally a matter of the quality of underwriting (terms, collateral, covenants, etc.).

When applying the credit rating definitions to individual loans, examiners should remember that ARIF is a type of secured lending. Decisions on risk ratings must take into account whether sources of repayment will produce sufficient cash flow to service the debt **as structured,** collateral value, and collateral liquidity. Any laxity in the bank's monitoring and control of the collateral can diminish the protections afforded by collateral and lower a loan's risk rating. Inappropriate structure can also be a significant factor in assigning an adverse risk rating.

Borrowers whose loans are administered in dedicated ARIF units, particularly asset-based lending[1] (ABL) units, often have high leverage and/or erratic earnings or losses. These characteristics are often the norm for ARIF borrowers; their presence does not necessarily warrant an adverse risk rating, but may do so if conditions deteriorate further.

More pertinent to the loan's rating is comparison of the borrower's actual performance with what was expected when the loan was underwritten. If the borrower repeatedly fails to meet earnings projections, has a trend of heavy losses or excessive leverage, needs internally approved over-advances too frequently or for too long, fails to provide timely financial information (including inventory and receivable aging information) fails to perform on related debt, or unexpectedly needs to access debt outside the ARIF line, the loan is a candidate for an adverse risk rating. An adverse rating may also be appropriate if the bank must adjust advance rates or change definitions of eligibility, including the addition of fixed assets to the borrowing base, to keep the loan within formula (see glossary). If liquidation of collateral (e.g., a forced sale by the bank or borrower), is an ARIF loan's most likely source of repayment, the loan would normally be classified as substandard at best.

Some industry participants contend that ARIF loans, especially those administered in well-controlled ABL units, should be assigned a more favorable risk rating than a loan with similar earnings and balance sheet characteristics because of the existence of collateral and the dedicated staff's oversight. Such a blanket system of applying risk ratings is not appropriate — in the same way that it is not appropriate to assign an adverse risk rating simply because an ARIF borrower has low or deficit net worth or occasional losses. While proper controls help to moderate the risk of asset-based lending, they do not by themselves overcome well-defined credit weaknesses.

Additional guidance on risk rating ARIF loans is provided in appendix C, which includes examples of adversely rated credits and the ratings' rationale.

---

[1] A specialized form of ARIF in which lenders exercise close control over credit availability and collateral by setting a borrowing base, controlling cash receipts, and carrying out field audits.

Types of Accounts Receivables and Inventory Financing

Because ARIF has many possible structures, the banking industry has many different definitions. This booklet divides ARIF into four types based on the level of monitoring and control. Regardless of the specifics of each category, examiners should focus on whether the monitoring and controls are adequate for the types of ARIF lending conducted by the bank. The four categories are defined as follows:

Asset-Based Lending (ABL) — A relationship in which lenders closely control credit availability and collateral. Asset-based lenders use a borrowing-base formula (derived by multiplying the value of eligible collateral by an advance rate or discount factor), control cash receipts, and carry out field audits. Borrowers often require daily loan advances to operate their businesses and lenders make daily adjustments to the available credit. Collateral consists predominately of accounts receivable and inventory. Because greater emphasis is on collateral (than in cash flow lending), ABL is structured so that collateral will be readily available if the loan must be liquidated. ABL is sometimes referred to as "commercial finance" or "fully followed" lending.

Secured Financing — Lending against a borrowing-base formula with less rigorous collateral controls and monitoring than in ABL. Loan advances are less frequent than in ABL. Although collateral is primarily accounts receivable and inventory, other kinds of assets also underpin the loan. The lender's controls generally consist of periodic accounts receivable agings, periodic inventory reports, and occasional field audits. The loan and security agreement normally require a properly authorized corporate officer to submit periodic certifications attesting to the accuracy of the borrowing base information. The borrower has greater control of the collateral than in ABL and usually has full access to the cash receipts. Borrowers are usually stronger financially than in ABL, enabling the bank to ease administrative controls.

Blanket Receivables Lending — Asset-types other than accounts receivable and inventory that are often included in the collateral pool. Advances are not tied to borrowing-base formulas. Controls are minimal, and monitoring of the collateral is informal. Collateral valuations may be based on financial statements.

Factoring — The lender purchases receivables outright, with or without recourse.

Although any loan with a lien against current assets, such as a blanket receivables loan, is technically ARIF, this booklet is primarily concerned with arrangements in which lenders closely monitor and control collateral. However, many of the issues discussed in this booklet, including those related to collateral valuation and quality, are relevant for examiners evaluating other, less-controlled loans secured by liens on receivables and inventory. This is especially true if the loan appears likely to develop into a problem situation.

The following sections of the booklet describe how ARIF loans are underwritten and managed. The booklet distinguishes further between the practices of ABL, secured financing, and blanket receivables lending. (See appendix A for the characteristics of each type.)

Accounts Receivable and Inventory Financing Structures

Since ARIF loans can be structured in many different ways, lenders should understand what structure is best suited to the characteristics of the borrower's business. For example, should the loan be long-term or seasonal? Should it be "fully followed" or "desk-followed" (see glossary)? The purpose of the loan, the anticipated source of repayment, the creditworthiness of the borrower, and the cash operating cycle of the business will help determine the structure of an ARIF loan.

ARIF lenders will sometimes extend loans secured by fixed or other assets. They may even make unsecured loans. These loans may be separate agreements or part of complex "structured" loan agreements. The term "structured finance" is used to describe an arrangement that has more than one layer or type of debt. (Structured finance is discussed in this booklet's "Specialty Financing Arrangements" section.) ARIF lending structures commonly include revolving credit, "permanent" working capital, seasonal operating advances, over-advances, and term debt.

Revolving Credit

A revolving line of credit (revolver) is the most common type of ARIF loan. A revolver normally supplies working capital. Cash from the conversion of inventory and receivables repays the debt. The loan agreement defines the amount of control the lender will have over the collateral and cash proceeds. Examiners should determine whether the necessary controls exist and whether they are properly exercised.

Generally, the borrower is expected to apply cash-collateral proceeds to the revolver, but some secured lending arrangements are underwritten with the understanding that the borrower can use cash-collateral proceeds for other purposes without first applying proceeds against the revolver. Because such arrangements pose greater risk, the lender should have stronger controls. For example, the bank might obtain borrower certifications and carry out periodic field audits.

In a typical revolver, a borrower can draw against the credit as many times as needed up to the lesser of the available borrowing base or the note amount. The loan amount outstanding fluctuates with the cash needs of the borrower, subject to the availability constraints of the borrowing base. Credit availability is restored when the borrower makes principal payments or borrowing base collateral is augmented. For the credit to remain available, a borrower must comply with terms and conditions stipulated in the loan agreement.

The terms of a revolving credit facility can vary considerably. Maturities, which are usually from one to three years, have recently been extended to as many as five years. A demand feature and other discretionary controls allow the lender considerable flexibility and control. Some revolvers are converted to term loans after a specified period. Revolvers may also contain sub-limits or over-advance provisions to meet specific needs of the borrower.

"Permanent" Working Capital

"Permanent" working capital loans, which fund business operations, new growth, acquisitions, and other general purposes, make up much of an ABL unit's core business. The unit makes what is more akin to an injection of equity capital than a loan; the borrower is usually highly leveraged and relies on the value of the pledged collateral to support the added credit risk. The ABL unit does not expect the borrower to amortize such a loan from operating cash flow. Permanent working capital is that portion of a revolver that is not repaid annually. Such debt is sometimes described as "evergreen" because it is not repaid until the company refinances the debt, liquidates, or is sold.

Ideally, the borrower will eventually build enough equity capital — through profitable operations, additional equity injections, or both — to no longer need such financing. In many cases, however, the borrower is unable to repay the layer of "permanent" debt and the debt is refinanced. Examiners should make sure that any rewriting of a loan is warranted; refinancing should not be a way to avoid recognizing a problem.

Lenders generally extend permanent working capital loans because they recognize that the borrower's capital base can support additional leverage. However, the desire to enhance return on equity may motivate some borrowers to assume unsupportable debt levels. Examiners need to evaluate whether the amount of debt is prudent given the inherent risk in the business and the borrower's ability to pay.

At times, lenders extend permanent working capital loans to help a borrower recover from an unplanned event. An unexpected business or economic downturn may interfere with the borrower's repayment of a seasonal advance, or an accident may not be adequately covered by insurance. In such circumstances, lenders rely on the ability of the borrower's management to restore the company's repayment capacity. Lenders need to objectively evaluate that capacity before extending additional credit. Examiners should make similar assessments. It **may** be appropriate to assign a special mention or substandard risk rating to a working capital loan extended because of an unplanned event.

The condition of the borrower's industry, that industry's stage in the industry cycle, the collateral support, and the level of controls and monitoring affect repayment expectations for permanent working capital debt. For example, borrowers in immature industries experiencing rapid growth may require "permanent" working capital loans for longer periods until their revenues stabilize and cash flows can be dedicated to debt repayment. Unlike the ABL lender, other secured lenders should expect the borrower to repay a permanent working capital loan from operating cash flow. The cash flow should support amortizing this debt over a reasonable period, usually five to seven years.

Often an ARIF lender will separate the debt into permanent working capital and a traditional revolver with a "clean-up" requirement. At certain designated times, the borrower is expected to "clean up" (that is, repay) the revolver and maintain the line at a zero balance. Typically, the clean-up is timed to coincide with the low point in the borrower's operating cycle and extends for at least 30 consecutive days annually. Alternatively, the borrower may be required to reduce the revolver to a designated "low point" for a specified period of time.

Lenders should convert stagnant permanent working capital loans to amortizing loans that will be repaid from operating cash flow. Loans to borrowers that do not have sufficient operating cash flow to fully amortize the permanent working capital debt represent a significant credit weakness. Depending on the collateral coverage, such loans may be classified from substandard to loss.

Borrowers that need "permanent" working capital loans are high risk and require the intensive supervision of a dedicated ABL unit to control such risk. When examiners see this type of lending outside an ABL unit, they should evaluate whether the bank has the resources and experience to provide adequate supervision. Improperly supervised "permanent" working capital loans may warrant criticism or classification. A possible exception to the high risk characterization of permanent working capital loans is a borrower who has undergone rapid growth and then begins to stabilize. In such cases, the lender may elect to divide the loan between the ARIF line and an amortizing term loan representing the longer term working capital needs of the borrower.

Seasonal Operating Advances

For many businesses such as apparel manufacturers and retailers, demand is seasonal. At certain times of the year, they require additional working capital. Before a peak-selling season, apparel manufacturers borrow to finish goods and build inventory levels. As inventory is sold, receivables increase until payments become due. Retailers often borrow to increase store inventory before heavy selling periods, such as holiday or tourist seasons, and repay after those seasons. A borrower may also need temporary inventory financing when a key supplier offers a special promotion.

"Seasonal" credit advances are tied to the operating cycle of the specific business, the product of the borrower, or both. Lenders can structure a seasonal operating advance as a single-maturity note or a sub-limit option within a revolver. However, loans drawn under a revolver may not be specifically identified as seasonal. To distinguish the seasonal and "permanent" portions of a line, examiners should perform an operating cycle analysis (see page 15) and review historical line usage and repayment patterns. Examiners should also review quarterly financial information to evaluate working asset account volumes and borrowing levels. For borrowers that expect to grow, lenders and examiners should review pro forma balance sheet and income statements. Significant deviation from pro formas usually warrants further analysis and may signal a potential problem.

Lenders expect borrowers to repay seasonal advances in full by the end of the seasonal business cycle, normally by converting the supporting collateral into cash. Failure to repay seasonal advances on time may indicate a significant credit weakness. To assess whether a credit weakness exists, examiners should review trends in the borrower's sales and profit margins; trade cycle trends, including trends in receivable, inventory, and payable turnover ratios; and overall operating cash flow relative to debt service and ongoing operating requirements. Examiners should also determine the reason for any departure from historic borrowing patterns. If a borrower's financial performance is clearly weak, the loan should receive an adverse risk rating, even if collateral protection seems adequate. Unless reversed, financial deterioration often decreases underlying collateral values and increases exposure to loss. Exceptions to an adverse rating should be rare and would be appropriate only when the collateral is of high quality and the debt is substantially below the borrowing base or the loan was advanced under bankruptcy approved DIP (debtor-in-possession) financing.

Over-advances

Over-advances are loan advances that exceed the borrowing base. Although over-advances normally have the same priority lien status as other loan advances, they represent increased credit risk because collateral protection is reduced. Like any other new extension of credit, an over-advance should be approved in accordance with the bank's loan policies. Even when properly approved, frequent or longstanding over-advances are a sign of credit weakness.

The credit approval documents of many ABL units and some secured lenders explicitly state when and under what conditions the lender will permit an over-advance. Such documents should stipulate the amount, frequency, duration, and period of the year when over-advances are permitted. Over-advances should be modest in amount and frequency; most important, they should have a defined repayment plan. Most lenders do not allow over-advances in excess of 10 percent of the borrowing base. Lenders should also do their best to verify that the borrower is using the proceeds as designated rather than masking obsolete inventory or slow sales.

Lenders commonly permit over-advances for:

Seasonal Inventory Buildup — Borrowers may have brief periods during their normal operating cycle when inventory buildup exceeds sales. In these situations, the lender may temporarily increase the inventory advance rate to accommodate an over-advance. For example, lawn and garden equipment manufacturers may require additional credit availability during the winter months when sales are slow and inventory is accumulated for spring shipments.

Acquisition Finance — Borrowers also use over-advances to accommodate acquisitions. Such over-advances should be placed on prudent amortization schedules. Extended maturity schedules and heavy skewing of repayments toward the latter years may expose the bank to unwarranted risk. Examiners should determine whether the lender is carefully reviewing pro forma consolidated financial information at the time of the acquisition and during the life of the loan to ensure that projections are in line with historical performance. Often lenders do not have as much control over these loans as over traditional ARIF loans. If a lender permits over-advances to be used in acquisitions, its control over receivables and inventory should be commensurate with the leverage in the post-merger balance sheet.

Unplanned, Approved Over-advances — At times, borrowers will need an over-advance because their borrowing base shrinks without a corresponding increase in cash flow. The borrower's receivable collections may slow, sales may decline, or inventory may be written down. If the borrower requests an over-advance, the lender must decide whether to adjust the borrowing base or, in some instances, advance additional funds. Alternatively, the lender may require the borrower to find other sources of financing or undertake an orderly liquidation of the collateral. If the lender chooses to support the borrower, the lender should structure a repayment plan to clear the over-advance as quickly as possible.

Unplanned, Unapproved Over-advances — A borrower rarely lacks sufficient time to inform the lender that an over-advance is likely to occur and to request an accommodation. When unapproved over-advances occur, either repayments are not adequate to meet a decline in the borrowing base (usually because cash flows have been diverted to build inventory, purchase fixed assets, pay dividends, or fund distributions) or the borrower has misrepresented the collateral.

Although an unapproved over-advance cannot be recalled, the lender should immediately develop a strategic response. Since the borrower is in default, the lender can demand repayment, renegotiate the terms of the loan, or even liquidate the collateral. Renegotiation affords the lender the opportunity to add collateral, guarantor support, or collateral controls.

Unplanned, unapproved over-advances reflect a serious credit weakness because they suggest deficiency in the borrower's repayment capacity, character, or both. If a bank repeatedly ignores over-advances, it jeopardizes its right to declare default later. Examiners should criticize such lax credit risk management practices.

Term Debt

Banks frequently make term loans to their ARIF borrowers. Traditionally term loans financed capital expenditures and the financed assets secured them. However, both the purpose and structure of term debt have changed. Term debt may or may not be part of a structured finance transaction that combines ARIF with other secured and unsecured credits.

Before extending term debt, lenders should determine that cash flows are adequate to service both the term debt and the ARIF line. Examiners should be aware that even when term debt is well structured and has adequate collateral coverage, such debt can increase the risk in the ARIF line. For instance, when a borrower's financial condition is deteriorating, a term loan may call for a different collection strategy than the one used for an ARIF line. Lenders may hesitate to liquidate the ARIF line if doing so could jeopardize the recovery on the term debt. Additionally, when a loan has cross-collateral and cross-default features, the line's collateral can be extended to cover partially secured facilities and the line can itself become under-secured.

Some lenders make term loans to cure over-advances. Over-advances are usually corrected by collecting receivables or selling down inventory. A borrower that needs to "term out" an over-advance often has serious financial problems. Although properly structured term loans can help a qualified borrower through a short-term over-advance problem, a lender should not use term debt to defer recognizing a problem. A loan to term out over-advances should have a short payout (usually not more than 12 months), documented borrower repayment capacity, and adequate collateral coverage. If it does not, the debt should usually be classified.

When a borrower has loans with more than one unit of a bank, one of the units should be assigned responsibility for the entire relationship. The relationship will be easier to monitor and the borrower will be treated consistently. Normally, because of the special requirements associated with ARIF, the ARIF unit is best equipped to be the responsible unit and to control the risk.

When an ARIF borrower has credit relationships with other financial institutions, it becomes more difficult to monitor the relationship. Many lenders include a covenant in ARIF loan agreements that prevents borrowing at other institutions without the ARIF unit's knowledge and consent. Prudent lenders will specifically prohibit ABL facilities at other institutions because of the control issues associated with shared collateral. But an ARIF lender may not object to other types of borrowing and may want to confine its exposure to the asset-based loan, which has tight controls limiting the risk of loss in the event of default. For example, the lender may be comfortable with another lender providing specialized financing, equipment leasing, and mortgages.

Evaluating the Borrower

An ARIF lender must analyze the financial condition of an ARIF borrower just as completely as it would any other commercial borrower. But for ARIF, the analysis of repayment capacity is centered in the borrower's cash flow from receivables and inventory, rather than cash flow from operations. The examiner's analysis should place more importance on the quality and value of receivables and inventory, the adequacy of the bank's controls and monitoring systems, and the bank's ability to convert collateral to cash in distressed situations than on income and balance sheet information.

Because the quality of an ARIF loan depends so much on the collateral, lenders should thoroughly analyze the borrower's business and industry, the borrower's position within the industry, and the types of customers with whom the borrower does business. Understanding the borrower's customer base will help the lender determine the quality of the receivables and level of third-party credit risk.

Assessing the Borrower's Financial Position

ARIF borrowers can be large or small, be new companies or well-established firms, experience rapid growth or large seasonal fluctuations, have sound or weak profit margins, and come from many industries. But almost all ARIF borrowers share one characteristic — an inability to generate sufficient working capital over the business's operating cycle. They are often companies with positive working capital positions but insufficient cash or credit. Examples include companies with long production cycles, such as airplane manufacturers, or companies with unplanned build-ups of inventory. ARIF borrowers may also have:

Debt/equity leverage that is higher than the industry average. Such under-capitalization can have various causes. A company may have lacked capital since it was first organized, may be experiencing rapid growth, may be an aggressive acquirer, or may have experienced some large losses that depleted its capital reserves. Such a company does not usually have much access to capital markets.

Historical uneven income or cash flow streams. Such a company's industry is usually highly cyclical, its businesses are subject to regulatory pricing constraints, or its management adjusts too slowly to market changes.

Negative financial trends. Sometimes a bank will "convert" a company with a satisfactory balance sheet from a less formally monitored type of commercial loan to ARIF because of negative trends in the company's earnings, sales, or margins. The conversion affords the bank better control over the increasing risk, while providing the company with needed credit.

Exhibit 1　　　　　**Operating Cycle**

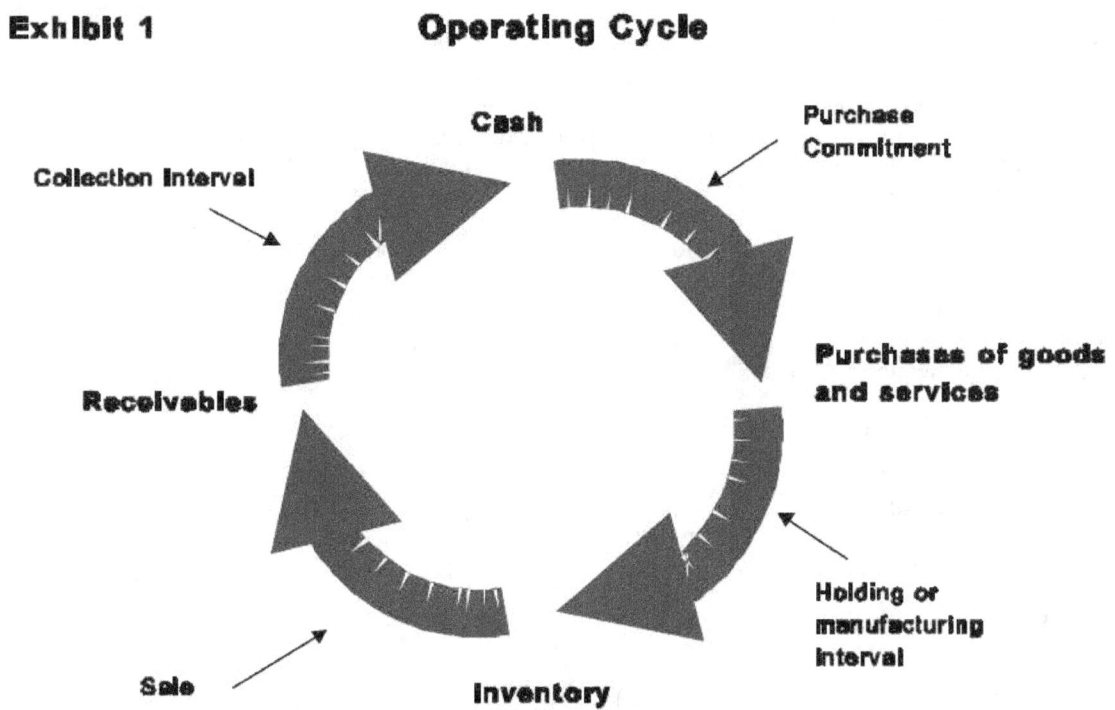

Assessing the Borrower's Operating Cycle

The lender's knowledge of the borrower's operating cycle enables it to structure a loan that fits the borrower's needs and protects its own interests.

The operating cycle (see exhibit 1) describes how long it takes a business to purchase goods or raw materials, convert those goods to inventory, sell the inventory, and collect the accounts receivable. Operating cycles vary from industry to industry depending on the length of the manufacturing process and the credit terms offered. A business must take into account how long after purchasing goods and services (cash outflow) it is able to convert its own goods and services into cash (cash inflow).

Suppliers of goods and services may provide some cash flow support by extending credit for purchases, creating accounts payable. And the business may be able to defer cash outlays for certain expenses (accrued expenses). The difference between cash flow needed during the holding and collection intervals and the cash flow provided by payables and accrued expenses is the net cash operating need, also referred to as the business's working investment need.

The working investment need is calculated in the following manner:

Exhibit 2   **ABC Company**

Balance Sheet (000s)

Cash	60	Notes Payable	75
Accounts Receivable	300	Accounts Payable	250
Inventory	500	Accrued Expenses	125
Other	40	Current Maturities LTD	150
Current Assets	900	Current Liabilities	600
Net Fixed Assets	1,000	Long-term Debt (LTD)	900
Other Assets	100	Equity	500
Total Assets	2,000	Total Liab. & Equity	2,000

Working Investment Availability

Accounts Receivable	300	
Inventory	500	
Op. Cycle Need		800
Accounts Payable	250	
Accrued Expenses	125	
Op. Cycle Provides		375
Working Investment Need		425

Some analysts prefer to calculate working investment needs in days instead of dollars to facilitate comparative and trend analysis. (See appendix B for further information.)

A business must maintain sufficient cash flow to meet its working investment need throughout the entire operating cycle. Well-capitalized and highly profitable businesses can often meet this need from internal operations. Businesses with less capital support, those experiencing rapid growth, or those with large seasonal demands may require external financing. In addition to repayment from converting working assets to cash flow, ARIF borrowers also generate needed cash from financing or refinancing of hard assets and from liquidation of assets.

Assessing the Borrower's Industry

A borrower's performance and collateral value are affected by conditions in the borrower's industry. For example, when the domestic automobile industry is in a downturn, the business of the parts manufacturers that supply it may slow, too. Although such a manufacturer may have an acceptable balance sheet, it may have to adjust for declining auto sales at the same time the auto manufacturers are putting pressure on its margins.

During a downturn, an entire industry will often extend the receivables collection period. By analyzing the industry, both the lenders and the examiners are better able to understand whether changes in a borrower's financial condition and operating cycle are due to the changes in the industry in general.

Assessing the Borrower's Management Team

Because companies that need ARIF are often leveraged, growing rapidly, or both, they need capable management. Not only does higher leverage reduce the margin for error, but a growing business has changing needs which can challenge even the most experienced management team. The borrower's management team, therefore, should be able to manage both current operations and expected growth. Lenders should evaluate the borrower's management team when the loan is made and at least annually thereafter.

Evaluating Collateral

Accounts Receivable

Whether an ARIF loan is a simple single advance note secured by a blanket lien on receivables and inventory or a fully followed asset-based loan, much of the collateral support is usually accounts receivable. Lenders need to conduct a thorough analysis of the receivables at origination and periodically thereafter.

Receivables' advance rates vary depending on the nature of the receivables. While banks usually advance amounts equal to between 70 percent and 80 percent of eligible receivables, lower advance rates may be warranted when there is heightened risk. Advance rates should take into consideration dilution trends, diversification, and the overall quality of the borrower's customer base (e.g., publicly rated companies, small privately owned companies, consumers). Examiners can evaluate advance rates on an individual loan by comparing them with those on other loans in similar industries and to the same borrower over time. Loans with advance rates that are higher than the industry norm or historical benchmarks have heightened risk. Examiners should evaluate the mitigants to the increased risk and assess the overall condition of the borrower. Banks often raise advance rates to try to accommodate a borrower's need for more working capital. By the same token, very low advance rates may also warrant added scrutiny. ARIF lenders, especially ABL lenders, will often reduce advance rates to build a collateral cushion if they feel that a liquidation may be imminent.

Much of a receivable's value (its collectibility) depends on the creditworthiness of the underlying customer. Therefore, an analysis of receivables usually begins with an evaluation of the financial strength of the borrower's customer base. In making this evaluation, examiners and lenders should consider:

Quality of customer base. In general, the greater the number of financially sound companies, the better the quality of the customer base. As the receivable base shifts toward smaller companies, financially weaker companies, or both, the risk increases that the borrower will not be able to collect the amounts it is owed. Consumer receivables are often considered higher risk because of the difficulty and higher costs in collecting many small receivables compared to collecting a relatively few large receivables.

To determine the financial strength of customers, lenders review available credit reports, trade checks, and debt ratings, or they conduct credit investigations themselves. This credit information should be readily available in the borrower's internal credit department. By reviewing the borrower's credit files, the lender can also make sure the borrower has a satisfactory internal due diligence process. After the lender or its field auditors analyze the borrower's customer base, the analysis should be documented in the credit file.

Concentrations. Like any credit portfolio, an ARIF customer base that has concentrations is riskier than one that doesn't. A concentration exists when a few customers produce the majority of receivables or when sales are primarily to customers in one industry. Given that many ARIF borrowers are manufacturers who sell specialty merchandise or are in the service sector and sell services to other businesses, receivables concentrations occur frequently. A receivables concentration of one account or a few large accounts is often referred to as "single-party" risk. If the "single party" takes its business elsewhere or its financial condition deteriorates, the borrower's business could be compromised. This risk is considerable if a borrower is unable to diversify.

Lenders normally consider receivables to be concentrated if there are single accounts representing 10 percent or more of the total receivables portfolio. Lenders extending credit to borrowers with a concentrated customer base should limit concentrated accounts to no more than 10 to 20 percent of the receivables borrowing base. Alternatively, they may reduce the percentage advanced against such concentrations. Exceptions to concentrations limits should be rare and based on unique circumstances that mitigate the concentration risk.

Lenders should consider the amount of risk posed by concentrations and structure the loan agreement to moderate such risk. In analyzing concentrations, the lender should consider the underlying credit quality of the account parties.

Delinquency status. Lenders should monitor delinquency trends within the accounts receivable base. Rising delinquencies indicate increased risk and may signal problems with the borrower. The effectiveness of the borrower's internal collection department will influence delinquency levels, but other factors, such as an increase in disputed accounts, can cause delinquencies to rise. Accounts that are past due 30 days or more beyond the normal trade terms are considered delinquent. Trade terms commonly call for full payment within 30 days of the invoice date, excluding any early payment discount offered. But certain industries have their own conventions. For example, the food industry usually requires payment in seven to 10 days. The normal practice is to consider accounts ineligible when they exceed three times the terms, e.g., 90 days for 30-day terms and 21 days for 7-day terms. In addition, most underwriting agreements specify that all accounts of a single party will be designated ineligible collateral when any (or some percentage) of that customer's receivables become ineligible. This is referred to as "cross-aging."

Dilution. ARIF borrowers and their lenders are exposed to dilution risk — the possibility that non-cash credits will reduce, or dilute, the accounts receivable balance. Returns and allowances, disputes, bad debts, and other credit offsets create dilution. While percentages vary by industry, dilution is usually 5 percent or less of receivables.

Lenders should analyze carefully trends or other significant changes in dilution rates. Field auditors should review and test selected credit memos. These reviews are important because a rise in dilution rates can signal a decline in product or service quality, which can lead to financial problems for the borrower.

Ineligible Collateral

ARIF loan agreements usually specify that certain receivables are ineligible as collateral because of the type of receivable or the delinquency status. The following types of receivables are usually considered ineligible:

- *Government receivables* because of the unique perfection and documentation requirements of the Assignment of Claims Act of 1940. Other possible reasons are: the government contractor or borrower may be subjected to strict specifications and rigorous inspections, the government entity may have liberal rights to return the goods, or the payment of government receivables often extends well beyond normal trade terms. If government receivables are eligible, the lender may permit a longer collection period. If so, the lender should have evidence that the primary government entity has established an acceptable payment pattern and that the borrower can meet the performance requirements of the contract.

- *Foreign receivables* because they have legal risks, foreign currency translation risks, and sovereign risks that can disrupt payment. If lenders allow such receivables to be eligible, they often require a letter of credit or an insurance policy carrying minimal deductibles.

- *Affiliate transactions* because the financial conditions of affiliates may deteriorate simultaneously. Affiliate receivables can also increase the potential for fraud, particularly in times of financial stress.

- *Contra-accounts* (when a borrower both sells to and purchases from the same customer) because the customer can "set off" the debt it owes against the debt owed to it and pay only the net amount.

Inventory

Banks should evaluate inventory, as they do receivables, in order to establish advance rates. Advance rates on inventory are usually lower than those on receivables because inventory is less liquid. Outstanding accounts need only be collected; goods in inventory must be finished, sold, and paid for. An additional risk factor in lending against inventory is the potential of a priority claim by the supplier of the inventory goods. In some industries and states the seller of the inventory may have an automatic prior lien (also known as a purchase money security interest) on that inventory even if there is no UCC filing.

Advance rates on inventory generally range between 20 percent and 65 percent. When establishing inventory LTV rates, lenders can limit risk by using the liquidation value (rather than the higher market value) of the inventory pledged and building in a sufficient margin to protect against price risk and marketing and administrative costs. To establish the value of various types of inventory, lenders should rely on expert appraisals or evaluations and their experience liquidating similar types of inventory.

Inventory advance rates vary depending on the inventory's product type and state, i.e., raw materials, work-in-process, or finished goods. Finished goods and commodity-like raw materials usually receive the highest advance rates because they are easiest to sell. Advance rates for some finished products such as fungible goods or goods with established markets are normally of greater value than specialized or perishable goods (unless such goods are adequately insured). As for raw materials, commodity items such as iron ore used by a steel maker are much easier to resell than customized items such as specialty pigments used to manufacture paint. Customized component parts may have only nominal resale value. Work-in-process is frequently excluded from the collateral used to determine the borrowing base because it has limited liquidation value since it requires additional production cost to be converted to salable merchandise.

Inventory must be salable to be considered eligible collateral. Some inventory should be excluded from collateral because of age or some other measure of obsolescence. Lenders should pay particular attention to borrowers in fashion-sensitive industries to ensure that obsolete inventory is written off in a timely manner. Eligibility may also be limited because of the location of the goods. For example, eligible inventory may be limited to goods located at the Anytown plant and exclude inventory held at the Central City plant. Inventory stored in multiple locations may be assigned a lower advance rate because it is more difficult to monitor and control and often is more costly to liquidate. Consignment goods are normally considered ineligible because they, too, are more difficult to control. Examiners should apply the same approach to inventory that they do to receivables: assess the reasonableness of advance rates by comparing such rates over time and reviewing trends in similar industries.

Although considerable reliance on inventory in the borrowing base may be appropriate depending on the nature of the borrower's business, ARIF loan borrowing bases are usually heavily skewed toward accounts receivable. Examiners should be particularly alert for a borrowing base's shift from reliance on accounts receivable to reliance on inventory. This is often a sign of financial deterioration and potential collection problems.

Additional Collateral

The collateral for some ARIF loans includes fixed assets such as equipment and real estate and may even include certain intangibles. Lenders who finance distressed companies or acquisitions are more likely to include this less liquid collateral when calculating the borrowing base. When they do, the agreement generally limits such collateral to a small percentage of the borrowing base. As much as possible, an ARIF loan should be supported by working assets. A separate mortgage loan should finance real estate for an ARIF borrower. However, when the ARIF lender is providing mortgage financing, the real estate loan may be cross-collateralized to cover any deficiency balance on the ARIF loan.

Underwriting ARIF Loans

Loan agreements are written, signed contracts between a borrower and a lender that clearly define the terms and conditions that govern the loan. In ARIF, the sections pertaining to collateral requirements are of prime importance. Other sections of the loan agreement address the legally binding conditions such as covenants, the existence and terms of any recourse or guarantee arrangements, the loan structure (revolving, term, etc.), maturity, and reporting requirements.

Collateral Controls in the Loan Agreement

The loan agreement should clearly identify the assets securing the loan — usually **all** receivables and inventory and sometimes equipment, real estate, intangibles such as patents and trademarks and other assets. Most ARIF loan agreements also establish what protections (e.g., insurance, inspections) the lender will require to protect the value of the collateral.

Most ARIF facilities are controlled, in part, through the borrowing base. The borrowing base limits the amount of funds that can be advanced under a revolving credit note at any particular time. The loan agreement establishes how the borrowing base is calculated by identifying the eligible types of collateral, defining the advance rates (LTVs) for each type of collateral, and setting sub-limits for certain types of collateral. For example, the agreement may state that inventory is limited to 30 percent of the total borrowing base and raw materials may not exceed 25 percent of inventory. The loan agreement also establishes how frequently the borrowing base is recalculated, identifies what documentation is necessary to support loan advances, and describes how cash proceeds are handled. The agreement also sets forth how the lender will verify the value of collateral and stipulates that the borrower will use advances in accordance with the loan agreement.

Collateral Liens

Collateral liens should be drafted as legally enforceable security interests in conformance with article 9 of the Uniform Commercial Code (UCC). Because of the continual turnover of receivables and inventory, the lender must use specific, enforceable language in the collateral documents to protect it from potential losses. The security agreement and the UCC filings should specify an interest in "existing and hereafter-acquired collateral, and all proceeds therefrom." To ensure the priority of the bank's lien position, the lender should conduct a lien search both before and after initial funding of an ARIF loan.

Ideally, one bank will be the exclusive lender against the receivables and inventory. However, sometimes a bank will make a loan against only a portion of a borrower's receivables or inventory and another lender will advance funds on the balance of those assets. These arrangements significantly increase risk because ownership and control of the collateral among the lenders can be uncertain. It is often impossible to clearly identify the secured interest in receivables among lenders when those obligations are due from common customers. Likewise, it is difficult to separate inventory among lien holders. A lender that accepts this additional risk should take precautions to make commingling of collateral difficult or impossible. At times, suppliers may file a purchase money security interest in raw materials or component parts. This, too, can compromise the collateral position of the lender.

Frequent field audits and detailed collateral descriptions can help reduce the risks, but the best solution is for a lender to ensure that it is the only lender to hold a lien against a firm's accounts receivable or inventory. When there are multiple lenders, they are often forced to resolve ownership issues through litigation. Not only must each lender absorb the expense of litigation but it may be forced to compromise with the other lenders in a manner that is not totally satisfactory to anyone.

Documentation

Collateral Appraisals

Many loan agreements authorize the lender to conduct formal written appraisals or evaluations of the pledged assets, in which a "market" and a "liquidation" (forced sale) value are assigned. Because these valuations help determine loan advances, only qualified, independent persons should perform them. The bank should maintain records describing the appraisers' qualifications.

Reporting Requirements

ABL units typically require annual audited financial statements from all their borrowers. Although many ARIF lenders do not require audited statements, all would benefit from their accuracy and detail. In secured financing and blanket receivables lending, the lender should evaluate the risks inherent in the specific credit relationship before deciding whether to require an audited statement. Bank policies or operating procedures typically address this subject.

Audited financial statements should be required when the lender relies on the financial statements to determine collateral values and when regular field audits are not required. Audited statements help the lender determine whether uncollectible receivables and obsolete inventory have been identified and appropriately reported on the balance sheet.

The frequency of financial reports should depend on how much credit risk the borrower poses. Although ARIF lenders should require such reports at least annually, most secured lending and ABL units require more frequent submissions (often monthly). Quarterly reporting is common in secured lending arrangements. ARIF borrowers are also required to certify compliance with the borrowing base and supply receivables agings quarterly, monthly, or even weekly. While borrowing base certificates and agings provide detailed information about the collateral, they are not a substitute for periodic financial statements.

The frequency of reports on inventory depends on the lender's assessment of the borrower's operations, the nature of the inventory, and the reliance on inventory in the borrowing base. Normally borrowers should be required to periodically certify the amount, type, and condition of their inventory; provide inventory valuations; and permit the lender or an independent firm to audit the inventory.

Abundance of Caution

Lenders will sometimes perfect a lien on receivables and inventory to support debt that is otherwise unsecured. Banks do so to provide a secondary source of repayment, to justify lower pricing, or to mitigate other factors such as concentration risk. Under these circumstances, the bank does not need to exercise the same degree of control and monitoring that it would for the more typical ARIF facility. Examiners should subject these loans to the financial analysis they would perform for other types of commercial loans and verify that the interest in the collateral is properly perfected and the valuation is reasonable.

If, however, financial analysis reveals that the assets under lien are the primary source of repayment, examiners should evaluate fully the receivables and inventory. Furthermore, absent proper controls, they should accord little weight to the receivables support when rating the loan's credit risk. If a bank has made a number of similar loans, examiners should criticize the bank's risk management and credit administration practices.

Financial Covenants

ARIF loan agreements normally include financial covenants that require the borrower to maintain or achieve certain financial ratios or levels of financial performance as an ongoing condition for the credit. Lenders should tailor the covenants to the specific risk profile of the borrower after analyzing the borrower's historical performance and projections. Covenants enable a bank to exercise control over those situations that pose heightened risk. They allow the bank to take certain defined and decisive steps to protect itself when certain performance levels are not achieved. Covenants do not exist simply to provide an early warning that the borrower's credit quality is deteriorating.

Typical ARIF financial covenants include:

- *Minimums* which address issues such as capital levels, income and cash flow coverage ratios, and working capital levels.

- *Maximums* which cover issues such as leverage ratios, capital expenditures, growth, dividends, and insider compensation.

Other types of covenants restrict asset sales, the assumption of new debt or equity, and the use of proceeds from these activities.

Lenders that waive a borrower's noncompliance with covenants undermine their controls and expose themselves to increased risk. Recently, many ABL units have been reducing the number of covenants in loan agreements. While a few meaningful covenants may be better than a "laundry list" of more detailed financial benchmarks, this approach has not yet been tested in an economic downturn. Lenders that limit the covenants in loan agreements may limit their ability to exercise additional controls over borrowers exhibiting increasing risk.

Third-Party Guarantees or Insurance

Third-party guarantees or insurance, a common feature of ARIF loans, are another way to reduce risk and may justifiably support higher LTV advance percentages. Nevertheless, they supplement, rather than replace, collateral controls.

Among the government-sponsored and private insurance programs are those that support foreign trade: the Export-Import Bank of the United States (EXIMBANK) and the Foreign Credit Insurance Association (FCIA), for example. Private insurance programs are also available to protect domestic receivables from loss; however, premium costs and restrictions on eligible receivables frequently limit borrowers' interest in these programs. These programs can significantly influence eligibility considerations and LTV advance percentages. Lenders should be aware of the requirements and restrictions of these programs, including any deductibles and whether the bank can be designated as loss payee.

Pricing

Traditionally, ARIF loans have produced higher yields than most other commercial loans. This is warranted because of the higher risk attributes of the borrower and the high administrative costs of monitoring and controlling ARIF loans. During the last decade competitive pressures have compressed the yields; however, ARIF loans, especially ABL, are highly profitable when losses are properly controlled.

Pricing for ARIF loans is based on a complex structure that combines fees, healthy spreads over cost of funds, and performance-based rates. Even today when most commercial loan pricing is based on LIBOR, many ARIF loans are still priced at a spread over prime. Loan agreements clearly establish conditions that trigger higher interest rates and fee-based servicing requirements. The fee structure typically includes customer charges for many of the administrative costs including field audit, lock box, and appraisals. Performance-based rate triggers include delinquency or dilution rates in excess of those specified in the loan agreement, violations of financial covenants, and over-advances.

Another source of added income in ARIF is the ABL practice of charging interest and fees to the revolver instead of collecting those payments in cash. The advantage to the lender is the ability to collect additional interest on those balances. This practice of "capitalizing" interest and fees is considered a sign of financial weakness in most types of commercial lending and a "well-defined weakness" that would warrant classification. However, as this is a longstanding and normal practice in ABL lending, it is not of itself a cause for an adverse risk rating.

Administering ARIF Loans

The complexity of administering ARIF loans results in higher transaction risk than for most other types of commercial loans. ARIF departments should be structured with a distinct separation of duties between credit approval, collateral/cash proceeds control, field audit, and portfolio management staff. Lending units that allow employees to perform conflicting roles can increase the bank's transaction risk.

The administration of ARIF loans is integral to controlling both credit and transaction risk. The loan agreements are complex, particularly with regard to collateral requirements, and compliance with administrative requirements is labor-intensive. To be successful, an ARIF program must have an experienced, adequately staffed back-office. Examiners should evaluate whether the staff is sufficiently trained and experienced to perform their responsibilities. Examiners should also review the quality of internal controls and audit systems. Because the overhead costs of properly administering ARIF can be high, some banks may be tempted to cut costs in this area. Examiners reviewing banks with smaller volumes of ARIF loans should pay particular attention to the adequacy of staffing, controls, and monitoring systems.

ARIF should be supported by strong management information systems (MIS) that can accurately compile and track information. Reports should be timely and factual. Good MIS enables ARIF lenders to identify over-advances and changes in borrowing patterns or collateral quality; it enables them to quickly take measures to control the risk. The examiner should evaluate the lender's systems against the range of risks assumed. For example, a lender making credit advances through a blanket receivable and inventory lending arrangement will not need the reporting systems and operational controls over collateral and cash proceeds that an ABL lender does.

Disbursing Revolving Loan Advances

ARIF lenders can choose from many systems for controlling the disbursement of loan proceeds and monitoring collateral. The goal is to safeguard the lender if the borrower defaults. Which process is best depends on the size of the lender's portfolio and the risk profile of the individual customer.

ABL units commonly exert strict control over the use of loan proceeds. Fully followed lines are the most tightly controlled. For such lines, funds are advanced against specific supporting collateral documents (such as invoices, shipping documents, or receipts) that are verified and reconciled during field audits.

Some borrowers draw against the available borrowing base rather than against specific supporting collateral documentation. Because this type of revolving arrangement gives the lender less control over the loan proceeds, the lender should keep track of borrowing activity so that it can investigate any unusual activity. Borrowing patterns should conform closely to the buildup of inventory and collection of receipts as reported on the borrowing base certificates. Borrower-prepared cash flow projections should detail expected borrowing needs and repayment activity. Examiners should ascertain how much control the bank exercises over loan disbursements.

Monitoring Systems

Monitoring can mitigate some of the risks of ARIF by ensuring that adequate margins are maintained. Receivables and inventory levels tend to fluctuate; an effective monitoring system allows a lender to continually update how much collateral exists and what its value is.

Lien Status Monitoring

Bankers should ensure that collateral liens are properly perfected and maintained. For example, bankers overseeing ARIF collateral need a tickler system to alert them to file continuation statements for financing statements (UCC filings), which expire after five years. If they do not "continue" the statements, the lender's security interest is at risk. The lender should also conduct periodic lien searches, particularly for its higher risk borrowers. Lien searches will disclose any other parties that have filed a security interest in collateral. It is especially important to uncover purchase money interests and tax liens, because they can take priority over the lender's lien.

Lock Box and Direct Deposit of Cash Collateral Proceeds

In most ABL and some secured financing relationships, the lender controls the borrower's cash receipts. Payments are made or transferred to the lender or to a lock box controlled by the lender. Some lenders notify the borrower's customers that they will control payments; most lenders do not. Payment by lock box benefits both the lender and borrower. The lender is able to monitor receivables and their cash flows continuously, and fraud risk is reduced. The borrower's account receives credit more quickly for receivables payments and the bank assumes some of the borrower's bookkeeping tasks.

Monitoring Receivables

Monitoring receivables is labor-intensive. Bank personnel need to verify borrower compliance with the loan agreement; identify trends in receivables quality, turnover rates, and concentrations; and update credit availability.

In ABL and some secured financing, lenders will require an aging of receivables which lists receivables by customer name, balance outstanding, and current payment status. Each day (or less frequently if the agreement so stipulates), the lender adjusts the maximum amount of credit available based on the amount of eligible receivables and cash receipts. Lenders should review the borrowing base revisions and loan outstandings to make sure the borrower is conforming to limits. If the borrower is not required to submit documentation supporting such conformance but only to certify compliance, the bank should have a system to ensure that "compliance certifications" are received by the due dates. The accuracy of compliance certifications is reviewed during field audits. Lenders secured by blanket assignment of receivables need to conduct timely reviews of financial information to determine the current level of collateral support.

Monitoring Inventory

Inventory can become obsolete and can build to excessive levels. Both of these situations adversely affect the marketability of the inventory, the financial condition of the borrower, and the collateral position of the bank.

The causes of excess inventory can be beyond the borrower's control (economic downturns), within the borrower's control (overly optimistic sales forecasts), or a combination of both (failure to react appropriately to competition from a new entity or product line). Inventory usually becomes obsolete when better products enter the marketplace. Although obsolescence risk can affect virtually any business, the risk is higher when product life cycles are shorter (in such industries as apparel and electronics).

Write-downs of excess and obsolete inventory affect the borrower (lower profits) and the bank (lower collateral value). If a write-down is significant, and it frequently is, capital and liquidity can come under pressure and a revolver can become over-advanced. Bankers and examiners should carefully analyze a borrower's switch from either FIFO to LIFO or LIFO to FIFO inventory accounting, because this practice can conceal inventory and operating problems.

Field Audits

Field audits are integral to controlling and monitoring ARIF. They help detect fraud and financial weakness. They are a standard way to confirm the quality of the borrower's financial data, receivables and inventory, and internal controls.

To ensure that financial reports are accurate, field auditors should obtain written account verifications and perform sufficient reconciliations and testing to ensure that the borrower's financial records are accurate. Testing financial records involves reviewing ARIF collateral: physically inspecting it, testing its validity and value as reported on financial statements and borrowing base certificates, and examining original invoices and other supporting documentation. During the field audit, the auditor should carefully review credit memo documentation, testing for both reasonableness and accuracy. Field audits are usually the best means of evaluating internal controls, information systems, and operating systems. The audits should confirm that the borrower's accounting systems are adequate. Some lenders require independent audited opinions of the borrower's operating systems and internal control systems.

Field audits should be conducted before a new account is booked and regularly thereafter — at least annually and, if risk dictates, quarterly or monthly. In a high-risk relationship or workout situation, weekly audits may be appropriate. Examiners should review how the bank determines the frequency and scope of field audits. They should pay special attention to ARIF units that delay audits or extend audit cycles because of staffing shortages. ABL units should have dedicated field audit staffs that include certified public accountants.

Banks that do not have field audit units should still inspect collateral and review supporting documentation periodically. Some banks have lenders perform audits; others out-source.

Covenant Monitoring

Banks require borrowers periodically to certify in writing that they are complying with the loan covenants. ARIF borrower compliance should be carefully monitored. Monitoring can give early warning of a change in the borrower's financial condition, and the compliance certificates often contain the borrowing base data for loan advances.

When a borrower fails to comply with loan covenants, lenders should carefully analyze the violations to determine the root cause and the implications for risk. The borrower and the lender should always acknowledge the violation and take appropriate corrective action. Lenders who fail to enforce covenants or who fail to clearly document the reasons for waivers may find that a court will invalidate the covenants and the rights they afford the bank.

Fraud

Fraud is a leading cause of loss in both secured lending and ABL. Regular collateral monitoring and timely field audits are the best deterrent to fraud-related losses. Since fraud can significantly reduce collateral values, lenders should make sure they do not advance funds against collateral that does not exist or never existed. A fraudulent borrower can submit falsified sales and collection documentation, use the same receivables as collateral to obtain financing from more than one lender, divert cash or collateral proceeds, misrepresent purchase orders, or overstate inventory levels.

Specialty Financing Arrangements

Certain types of ARIF have unusual risks and other unique characteristics. Lenders should have the appropriate management, staff, and monitoring systems for the types of ARIF they offer.

Structured Finance

Over the years bankers have developed certain loan products to moderate the risk of lending to highly leveraged borrowers. In recent years, structured finance loans have served this purpose, particularly for acquisitions. Receivables and inventory are often part of the collateral package.

Structured finance loans have two or more tiers (tranches) of debt. Maturities, amortization requirements, collateral, and pricing may vary from tranche to tranche. The most senior tier is normally a traditional revolver secured by receivables and inventory. Advances are subject to a borrowing base formula. Junior tiers are usually at least partially secured by fixed assets. As debt levels increase, collateral in junior tranches may be based on residual values (which produce more liberal advances than the customary formula); the business itself may secure the loan through a pledge of the company's stock — the so-called "enterprise" value. Examiners should keep in mind that such stock is "soft" collateral whose value can change quickly with changes in the borrower's financial condition, the borrower's industry, or the economy in general. (Refer to Advisory Letter 99-4 for a more complete discussion of enterprise values.)

Although structured finance loan agreements differ in detail, most agreements have cross-collateral and cross-default provisions that extend across the structure's tiers. If debt is liquidated, the "harder" values of receivables and inventory will be commingled with the "softer" values of fixed assets and stock. So, what appears to be a well-secured tier of debt may contain significant loss exposure if a default occurs. Examiners should incorporate the entire leveraged lending structure in their analysis of the structure's repayment capacity and collateral support. Structured finance loans are often far riskier than pure ARIF loans.

Debtor-in-possession Financing

Debtor-in-possession (DIP) financing is extended following a chapter 11 (reorganization) bankruptcy filing. DIP loans are under the close supervision of the bankruptcy court. Although some larger banks have special DIP financing units, many lenders provide such financing through ARIF departments.

If properly structured, documented, and administered, DIP financing should not pose undue credit risk. In fact, because of the protections afforded by bankruptcy laws, some lenders feel DIP financing has less risk than conventional ARIF. DIP financing helps protect the value of the collateral by allowing the bankrupt business to continue as a going concern. Strict ABL controls and monitoring are central to DIP risk management. Before engaging in this type of financing, a lender should seek the guidance and representation of an experienced bankruptcy attorney. The bank should also ascertain whether:

- The reorganization plan is likely to be approved by the courts.
- The lender is likely to receive repayment upon confirmation of the reorganization plan.

- The plan affords the lender collateral protection if the bankruptcy filing becomes a chapter 7 (liquidation) case.
- The plan assigns priority lien status to the post-petition DIP financing.

The lender should also consider whether more borrowing than the DIP financing and any pre-petition debt is likely.

It should be noted that lenders who do not participate in the DIP financing are normally left with inferior collateral, which is relegated to a second lien in favor of the DIP lender. Frequently this can be the fate of less sophisticated banks that lend on receivables and inventory but do not have the size or specialized experience to participate in the DIP financing.

Factoring

Factoring involves the direct purchase, usually without recourse, of third-party (traditionally termed the "customer") accounts receivable. The factor purchases the receivables at a discount, pays the company (traditionally termed the "client") what the third party owes, and assumes all the credit risk for the purchased accounts. There are two basic types of factoring: (1) discount factoring, in which the factor discounts the receivables prior to the maturity date, and (2) maturity factoring, in which the factor pays the client the purchase price of the factored accounts at maturity. Factors frequently perform all accounting functions in connection with the accounts receivable and purchasers are notified to remit payments directly to the factor.

Factoring is common in certain industries, particularly the textile industry. Generally factors will limit their activities to a few industries in which they have expertise and an established network. Although national banks can be factors, most factoring is done by nonregulated businesses.

A third-party "customer" does not have the same allegiance to the factor that it had to the seller of goods. Even when financially pressed, this party will pay a key supplier to ensure availability of critical goods. Nevertheless, a factor has some leverage and third parties are careful to cultivate the factor's support to protect their reputation and access to credit. The factor has the right to reject receivables from individual customers, and when this happens, the manufacturer is likely to reduce or halt sales to that customer.

Factoring is like ARIF in many ways; however, factors focus most of their due diligence on the third-party customer rather than the manufacturing "client."

Typically, the factor establishes an overall limit for the client and sub-limits for each third-party customer's receivables based on payment status, total exposure, and credit strength. Factors investigate client manufacturers to make sure that they have sufficient capacity to handle charge backs and disputed accounts. Factors also provide office support, conduct credit investigations, provide bookkeeping services, and collect receivables.

Factoring foreign receivables is more complex than factoring domestic ones because of the extensive trade documentation on foreign sales. The basic process is fundamentally the same: the factor purchases the receivables and assumes the position of the client, collecting the receivables as per the trade documents. Since the factor owns the drafts and documents, the collection process is undertaken for its account when documents are routed through a commercial bank. Occasionally, a factor will use its own credit line with a commercial bank to "carry" receivables purchased from the exporter until payment is received from the ultimate buyer. The factor may also act as an intermediary between its customer (the importer) and the bank by substituting its own credit for that of the importer. With the added support of the factor's guaranty, a bank may provide a letter of credit for a customer who may otherwise not meet the bank's credit standards. Please refer to the *Comptroller's Handbook* for more information about trade finance.

Third-Party Vendors

Some banks purchase computer software products from third-party vendors to assist them in providing receivables financing. These products are designed to support a factoring arrangement: the banks actually purchase receivables, usually with recourse. Although recourse protects against losses on individual receivables, the value of the recourse is only as good as the financial strength of the bank's client (seller of the receivable). The software provides the bank with a bookkeeping system to manage the receivables, and the vendor often assists the bank in acquiring customer accounts. The software, however, does **not** provide the lending and risk management expertise necessary to supervise this type of high-risk activity.

Bankers who purchase these products must have adequate knowledge of the risks in this type of financing and dedicate qualified staff to analyze the credit strength of the "clients" and monitor and control the receivables properly. Although the software can help with the monitoring and control of collateral and loan advances, the amount of assistance can vary considerably. Examiners should hold discussions with bank management to assess its knowledge of the business risks, especially in banks new to the business.

Although vendor products may be reliable, banks must still scrupulously manage ARIF credit risk and transaction risk. Examiners should carefully evaluate the implications for risk of each product. In addition, they should evaluate the bank's arrangements with outside vendors to ensure that the bank has appropriate controls and management expertise.

Compliance Issues

ARIF is subject to the same regulatory and compliance issues as other types of commercial lending. However, because of the dependence on collateral in trading accounts and the higher risk profile of the borrower, certain of these issues are more acute for ARIF.

Debt Liquidation and Lender Liability

Sometimes a bank must terminate funding and liquidate collateral because the customer is experiencing financial difficulties. Banks, however, should be careful about doing so, especially if the action could be considered abrupt, because courts have found lenders liable for contributing to the failure of a customer's business. Lenders should consult with counsel before taking action against a customer. And they should notify the borrower well in advance that its line of credit will be canceled (giving the borrower time to seek other sources of credit) or that its receivables and inventory will be liquidated. To prevent fraud after notifying a lender that financing will be terminated, the lender may have to intensify its monitoring, especially of inventory.

Because ARIF lenders normally supervise a borrower's business very closely, they can be vulnerable to lender liability suits whether or not they terminate funding or liquidate assets. Lending staff should have adequate training in lender liability and other compliance issues.

State and Federal Laws, Rules, and Regulations

ARIF lenders should keep abreast of the various state and federal laws and regulations that apply to their borrowers (see this booklet's "References" page).

For example, a lender should know how the laws on environmental contamination could affect a borrower. The bank's collateral can lose value if, for example, collateralized trade goods become contaminated. The borrower's financial position may become compromised if the borrower does not have the insurance to cover the cost of an environmental clean-up. In a number of cases, the courts have directed banks to pay to clean up contamination created by borrowers that lacked the financial ability to do so.

In ARIF, as in other types of commercial lending, safety, health, and fair labor laws and regulations that apply to the borrower are an indirect risk to the bank. If the borrower does not comply, it may have to pay fines or penalties, absorb clean-up costs, or expend capital to meet standards. These costs could compromise the borrower's financial position.

To control regulatory risks, banks should have a comprehensive compliance program that includes internal testing and training for their staffs. The program should cover the laws, rules, and regulations pertinent to ARIF borrowers. Lenders should also conduct a compliance review and environmental audit of certain borrowers as part of the due diligence and periodic inspection process. Lenders should determine whether the borrower's insurance policies are adequate.

Allowance for Loan and Lease Losses

For purposes of maintaining an adequate allowance for loan and lease losses (ALLL), the OCC encourages banks to segment their portfolios into as many components as practical. Banks may treat ARIF loans as a homogeneous pool for ALLL analysis or they may segment the portfolio into several pools based on industry concentrations or other characteristics.

Although loss experience for properly controlled ARIF borrowers is often less than for other commercial borrowers, an ARIF borrower's risk rating should be based on its risk of default. In many cases an ARIF loan may be designated substandard even though the amount of collateral and controls over the collateral appear to protect the bank from loss in the event of default. In these circumstances, the perceived lower loss potential should be accounted for in ALLL. Banks should ensure that their ALLL methodology accurately reflects their historical loss experience and other relevant factors. (For further guidance, see the "Allowance for Loan and Lease Losses" booklet of the *Comptroller's Handbook*.)

General Procedures

Objective: Develop the scope of the accounts receivable and inventory financing (ARIF) examination.

NOTE: These procedures should be used in conjunction with the more general procedures in the "Loan Portfolio Management" booklet and the *Comptroller's Handbook for National Bank Examiners.* The examiner conducting the ARIF examination should work closely with the LPM examiner to identify mutual areas of concern and maximize examination efficiencies. Much of the information required to perform these procedures will be available from the LPM examiner.

1. Read and discuss with the EIC the examination scope memorandum. Align the ARIF examination objectives with the goals of the examination. Assess resources allocated to the ARIF review in relation to your initial analysis of portfolio risk.

2. Review the following information in deciding whether previously identified issues require follow-up. In consultation with the EIC and LPM examiner, determine whether bank management has effectively responded to any adverse findings and carried out any commitments.

   ❑ Previous ROE.
   ❑ Bank management's response to previous examination findings.
   ❑ Previous ARIF examination working papers.
   ❑ Bank correspondence concerning ARIF.
   ❑ Audit reports and working papers, if necessary.
   ❑ Supervisory strategy, overall summary, and other relevant comments in the OCC's Electronic Information System.

3. Obtain from the EIC the results of the UBPR, BERT, and other OCC reports. Identify any concerns, trends, or changes in ARIF since the last examination. Examiners should be alert to growth rates, changes in portfolio composition, loan yields, maturities, and other factors that may affect credit risk.

4. Obtain from examiner assigned loan portfolio management and review the following schedules as applicable to this area:

- Loan trial balance, past dues, and nonaccruals for ARIF.
- Risk rating stratification reports, risk rating migration reports.
- Concentration reports and bank definitions of concentrations monitored.
- Exception reports.
- Problem loan status report for adversely rated ARIF loans.
- List of "watch" credits.
- Management reports used to monitor the portfolio, including reports:
    - Used to monitor compliance with the borrowing base.
    - On loans on which the borrowing base has been modified since the previous exam (by changing advance rates, adding types of collateral, liberalizing eligibility formulas, etc.).
    - On loans identified for intensified oversight or more frequent collateral auditing.
    - On loans with over-advances.
    - Listing borrowers who have received additional loans since receiving an ARIF loan.
    - On loans transferred to ARIF from other divisions within the bank.
- Specific ARIF policy guidelines.
- ARIF defined risk tolerance positions.
- Any useful information obtained from the review of the minutes of the loan and discount (or similar) committee.
- Reports related to ARIF that have been furnished to the loan and discount (or similar) committee or the board of directors.
- Report on fee income received from ARIF borrowers, including description of the nature of the fee.
- Loans on which interest is not being collected in accordance with the terms of the loan.
- Loans for which terms have been modified by a reduction of interest rate or principal payment, by a deferral of interest or principal, or by other restructuring of repayment terms.
- Loans on which interest has been capitalized after the initial underwriting.
- Participations purchased and sold since the previous examination.
- ARIF Shared National Credits.
- Miscellaneous ARIF debit and credit suspense accounts.
- Organization chart of the department.
- Resumes for ARIF management and senior staff.
- Each officer's current lending authority.

❑ ARIF profitability, capital usage, and budget reports.

5. Based on analysis of the information and discussions with management, determine whether there have been any material changes in the types of customer (based on product line), underwriting criteria, volume of lending, or market focus. Your analysis should consider:

❑ Growth and acquisitions.
❑ Management changes.
❑ Policy and underwriting changes.
❑ Changes in risk tolerance limits.
❑ Changes in external factors such as:
   - National, regional, and local economy.
   - Industry outlook.
   - Regulatory framework.
   - Technological changes.

Discussions with management should cover:
❑ How management supervises the portfolio.
❑ Any significant changes in policies, procedures, personnel, and control systems.
❑ New marketing strategies and initiatives.
❑ Any internal or external factors that could affect the portfolio.
❑ Management's perception of the ARIF credit culture.
❑ The findings of your review of internal bank reports on ARIF.

6. Based on performance of the previous steps, combined with discussions with EIC and other appropriate supervisors, determine the examination scope and how much testing is necessary.

7. As the examination procedures are performed, test for compliance with all applicable laws, rules, and regulations, and with established policies and processes. Confirm the existence of appropriate internal controls. Identify any area that has inadequate supervision or poses undue risk. Discuss with EIC the need to perform additional procedures.

Select from among the following procedures those necessary to meet the objectives. Examiners should tailor the procedures to the bank's specific activities and risks. All steps are seldom required in an examination.

Quantity of Risk

Conclusion: The quantity of risk is (low, moderate, or high).

Objective 1: Assess the types and levels of risk associated with individual ARIF loans and determine the appropriate risk rating.

1.   Select a sample of loans to be reviewed. The sample should be adequate to assess compliance with policies, procedures, and regulations; verify the accuracy of internal risk ratings; and determine the quantity of credit risk. The sample should also be used to test changes in underwriting, including borrowing base changes, and loans with over-advances. Refer to the "Sampling Methodology" booklet of the *Comptroller's Handbook* for guidance on sampling techniques.

2.   Prepare line sheets for sampled credits. Line sheets should contain sufficient information to determine the credit rating and support any criticisms of underwriting, servicing, or credit administration practices.

3.   Obtain credit files for all borrowers in the sample and document line sheets with sufficient information to determine quality, risk rating, or both. Assess how the credit risk posed by the financial condition of the borrower will affect individual loans and the portfolio. In your analysis:

   • Determine the disposition of loans classified or rated special mention during the previous examination.
   • Complete a thorough financial analysis of the borrower. Keep in mind that the primary focus with ARIF customers should be on analyzing the trade cycle. However, cash flows should be adequate to meet operating needs, including interest expense.
   • Determine whether the borrower complies with the loan agreement, including financial covenants and borrowing base requirements.
   • Evaluate the effect of environmental factors, such as economic conditions and the industry life cycle, upon the borrower's ability to repay.

- Determine, for seasonal operating advances or lines of credit, whether the trade cycle supports clean-up (complete payout) of that portion of the debt structure by the end of the normal business cycle.
- Determine, for permanent working capital loans, whether cash flow after other debt service, capital expenditures, and other operating needs is sufficient to amortize the debt within reasonable timeframes.
- Review any non-asset-based loans to determine whether cash flow is sufficient for debt service. Consider:
  - Working capital changes and needs.
  - Discretionary and nondiscretionary capital expenditures, product development expenses, and payments to shareholders.
  - The level of other fixed payments and maintenance expenses.
- Assess the obligor's access to capital markets or other sources of funds for potential support.
- Evaluate the loan agreement to determine:
  - Whether the loan structure is consistent with the borrower's needs and the business's operating cycle.
  - What collateral secures the loans and the accuracy of collateral descriptions, documentation and lien positions.
  - Advance rates against collateral (existence of borrowing base), collateral eligibility, LTV constraints, limits on concentrations, any borrowing base sublimits, frequency of calculations of the borrowing base, requirements for receipt of agings or lists of receivables, and field audit requirements.
  - Whether bank uses lockbox arrangement or direct deposit of cash collateral proceeds to control cash receipt and disbursement.
- Determine compliance with the above requirements of the loan agreement. If borrower is not in compliance, determine root cause and assess the impact on credit quality.

4. For the loans in the sample, assess the quality of the collateral support by:

- Reviewing results of any field audits performed in the previous year.
- Considering the financial strength of debtor accounts.
- Analyzing trends in dilution (disputes, returns, and offsets).
- Checking for concentrations in debtor accounts.
- Reviewing and testing the accuracy of eligible and ineligible receivables and comparing them with funds advanced under the agreed-upon LTV formula. Consider delinquencies, affiliate transactions, contra-party accounts, U.S. government receivables, and foreign receivables.
- Reviewing and assessing the valuation of inventory by:

- Considering potential impact of cyclical downturns, new competition, and overproduction that may result in excess, stagnant, or obsolete goods.
- Considering composition in terms of finished goods, goods-in-process, and raw materials.
- Determining presence of any functional obsolescence.
- Determining whether product type, product cycle, and specialty or perishable goods have been taken into account.
- Considering the method used to assign values.

5. Analyze any secondary support provided by guarantors and endorsers. If the underlying financial condition of the borrower warrants concern, determine the guarantor's or endorser's capacity and willingness to repay the credit.

6. Assess credit risk posed by the obligor's management team (specifically, by weaknesses in the team's quality, integrity, or ability to manage current operations and future growth) by determining whether:

    - Officer memorandums adequately address the ongoing quality, integrity, and depth of the borrower's management.
    - The bank has mitigated some of this risk by requiring key executives of the borrower to obtain sufficient life insurance policies payable directly to the bank, has loan covenants in place allowing the bank to reassess the borrowing relationship in the event of the loss of a key executive, or both.

7. Identify any policy, underwriting, and pricing exceptions in the loans sampled. If exceptions are not being accurately identified and reported, determine the cause and discuss with management. If warranted, commentary or schedules can be included in the Report of Examination.

8. Using a list of nonaccruing loans, test loan accrual records to determine that interest income is not being recorded.

9. Assign risk ratings to sampled credits. See "Risk Rating Considerations" in this booklet's "Introduction" for guidance.

Objective 2: Evaluate the effect of changes in underwriting standards, practices, and policies on the quantity of credit risk in the ARIF portfolio.

1. Review any changes to the ARIF loan policy and determine the effect on the quantity of risk.

2. Review the current underwriting guidelines or practices. Assess how changes since the previous examination may affect the quantity of risk. This should be done in conjunction with the sample of ARIF loans reviewed. Consider changes to:

    *   Advance rates,
    *   Collateral eligibility,
    *   Over-advances,
    *   The number and types of covenants,
    *   Maturities, and
    *   Financial reporting requirements.

3. Determine whether changes in processes have affected the level of risk in the portfolio. For example, if the frequency of field audits has been changed, determine how the change will affect credit risk.

4. Analyze the level, composition, and trend of ARIF underwriting exceptions. If this information is not available from bank MIS, develop it using the sample of loans taken during the examination. Determine whether the underwriting exceptions are increasing the level of risk within the portfolio or whether the exceptions are being properly mitigated.

5. If quantitative factors, such as delinquency, nonaccrual, adversely rated, average or weighted average risk rating have increased, try to determine any correlation with changes in underwriting policy or practice.

6. Evaluate how the ARIF strategic plan may affect credit risk, including the risk associated with rapid growth, geographic expansion, new or increased focus on borrowers in industries to which the unit had limited or no prior exposure, new products such as structured finance, etc.

Objective 3: Determine how the composition of the ARIF portfolio affects the quantity of risk.

1. Analyze the composition of and changes to the ARIF portfolio, including off-balance-sheet exposure, since the previous examination. Determine the implications for the quantity of risk of the following:

- Any significant growth.
- Material changes in the portfolio to include:
  - Changes and trends in watch, problem, classified, past-due, nonaccrual, and nonperforming assets; charge-off volumes; and risk rating distribution.
  - Loans with over-advances.
- Any significant concentrations, including geographic and product concentrations.
- Portfolios acquired from other institutions.

2. Review the portfolio to determine whether there has been any shift in the customer base that could increase risk. Such shifts might be to industries with which the bank has limited experience or to borrowers in foreign markets about which the bank has limited knowledge.

3. Analyze management-prepared ARIF portfolio risk assessments. Determine whether management's risk assessments are supported by the examiners' analysis of the loan sample.

4. Review the business and/or strategic plan for ARIF. Evaluate how implementation of the plan will affect the quantity of credit risk. Consider:

- Growth goals and potential sources of new loans;
- Growth outside the current market area;
- New products (e.g., vendor software) and business lines;
- Concentrations of credit; and
- Management's expertise, history, and experience with the plan's products and target markets.

5. Review the local, regional, and national economic trends and assess their impact on ARIF portfolio risk levels. Consider whether management has reasonably factored this data into projections of loan growth and quality.

6. Compare ARIF portfolio performance with planned performance and ascertain the risk implications.

7. If the bank employs concentration management tools (e.g., portfolio limits, loan sales, derivatives) to control credit exposures, analyze the impact on the quantity of risk. Consider:

- The objectives of these programs.
- Management's experience and expertise with these tools.

8. Review recent loan reviews of ARIF and any related audit reports. If there are any adverse trends in quantitative measures of risk or control weaknesses reported, comment on whether and how much they may increase credit risk.

9. Analyze the level, composition, and trend of documentation exceptions and determine the potential risk implications.

10. Evaluate the adequacy of the allowance for loan and lease losses for the ARIF portfolio.

11. Evaluate the transaction risk within the ARIF portfolio. Factors to consider include:

    • Product delivery systems.
    • Complexity of products.
    • Collateral monitoring requirements.
    • Adequacy of the bank's processes, systems, controls, and staffing relative to the volume and types of loans underwritten.

12. Evaluate the level of compliance with the laws, rules, and regulations listed on the "References" page of this booklet. Relate the level of compliance to the quantity of credit risk. Test for compliance as necessary.

13. If violations or noncompliance was noted, determine whether management took adequate corrective action.

Verification Procedures

Objective: Verify the authenticity of the bank's ARIF loans, and test the accuracy of records and adequacy of record keeping.

Note: Examiners normally will not need to do extensive verification. However, these procedures are appropriate when the bank has inadequate audit coverage of ARIF activities or when fraud or other irregularities are suspected.

1.   Test the additions of the trial balances and the reconciliation of the trial balances to the general ledger. Include loan commitments and other contingent liabilities.

2.   Using an appropriate sampling technique, select loans from the trial balance and:

    a.   Prepare and mail confirmation forms to borrowers. (Loans serviced by other institutions, either whole loans or participations, are usually confirmed only with the servicing institution. Loans serviced for other institutions, either whole loans or participations, should be confirmed with the buying institution and the borrower. Confirmation forms should include borrower's name, loan number, the original amount, interest rate, current loan balance, borrowing base, and a brief description of the collateral.)

    b.   After a reasonable time, mail second requests.

    c.   Follow up on any unanswered requests for verification or exceptions and resolve differences.

    d.   Examine notes for completeness and compare agree date, amount, and terms with trial balance.

    e.   In the event notes are not held at the bank, request confirmation by the holder.

    f.   Check to see that required initials of approving officer are on the note.

g. Check to see that note is signed, appears to be genuine, and is negotiable.

h. Compare collateral held in commercial loan files with the description on the collateral register.

i. Determine that the proper collateral documentation is on file.

j. Determine that margins are reasonable and in line with bank policy and legal requirements.

k. List all collateral discrepancies and investigate.

l. Forward a confirmation request on any collateral held outside the bank (e.g., by bonded warehouses).

m. Determine that each file contains documentation supporting guarantees and subordination agreements, when appropriate.

n. Determine that any required insurance coverage is adequate and that the bank is named as loss payee.

o. Review participation agreements, excerpting when necessary such items as rate of service fee, interest rate, retention of late charges, and remittance requirements, and determine whether participant has complied. Review disbursement ledgers and authorizations, and determine whether authorizations are signed in accordance with terms of the loan agreement.

3. Review field audits and:

a. Determine that on-site inspections are performed in conformance with bank policy.

b. Consider making a physical inspection of the collateral when the quality or frequency of the bank's inspection are not adequate.

c. If physical inspections are made, compare the results with the bank's records and investigate differences to the extent necessary.

4. Review accounts with accrued interest by:

a. Reviewing and testing procedures for accounting for accrued interest and for handling adjustments.

b. Scanning accrued interest for any unusual entries and following up on any unusual items by tracing them to initial and supporting records.

5. Using a list of nonaccruing loans, check loan accrual records to determine that interest income is not being recorded.

6. Obtain or prepare a schedule showing the monthly interest income amounts and the commercial loan balance at each month end since the last examination, and:

a. Calculate yield.

b. Investigate any significant fluctuations or trends.

Quality of Risk Management

Conclusion: The quality of risk management is (strong, satisfactory, weak).

Policy

Objective: To determine whether the board has adopted ARIF policies consistent with safe and sound banking practices and appropriate to the size, nature, and scope of the bank's operations and whether written underwriting guidance addresses important issues not included in board policies.

1. Evaluate the adequacy of ARIF policies and underwriting guidance. Policy or underwriting guidance should address:

   - The types of customers and industries that are acceptable.
   - Collateral guidelines, including:
     - Borrowing base components.
     - Advance rates on inventory and receivables.
     - Eligibility criteria.
   - Acceptable lending terms (on maturity, debt service coverage standards, if applicable, repayment plans, etc.).
   - Minimum standards for requiring, receiving, and analyzing financial data.
   - Standards for the frequency and accuracy of borrower certifications.
   - Procedures to monitor and enforce compliance with loan agreements.
   - Procedures governing the use of field audits, including their scope, timing, and frequency.
   - Procedures governing required follow-up on field audit deficiencies, including how the borrower should be required to respond to identified risks or deficiencies.
   - Procedures to properly perfect and maintain collateral liens.
   - How over-advances are approved.
   - Procedures governing the bank's control over cash and collateral proceeds, including use of lockbox arrangements.
   - Procedures for the use and monitoring of third-party guarantee or insurance programs.
   - Procedures for approving exceptions to policy and underwriting guidance and maintaining MIS to track those exceptions.

2.	Determine whether the policy establishes concentration guidelines for ARIF and outlines actions to be taken when limits are exceeded.

3.	Determine that annual reviews of ARIF policies and underwriting guidance are conducted by the board or an appropriate credit committee.

Processes

Objective: Determine whether lending practices, procedures, and internal controls regarding ARIF loans are adequate.

1.	Evaluate how policies, procedures, and plans affecting the ARIF portfolio are communicated. Consider:

- Whether management has clearly communicated objectives and risk limits for the ARIF portfolio to the board of directors and whether the board has approved these policies.
- Whether communication to key personnel in the ARIF department is timely.

2.	Determine whether management information systems provide timely, useful information to evaluate risk levels and trends in the ARIF portfolio.

3.	Assess the process to ensure the accuracy and integrity of ARIF data.

4.	Determine the effectiveness of processes to monitor compliance with ARIF policy. Consider:

- Approval and monitoring of policy limit and over-advance exceptions.
- The volume and type of exceptions including any identified in the loan sample.
- Internal loan review, audit, and compliance process findings.

5.	Assess the underwriting process for ARIF. Consider the appropriateness of the approval process and the adequacy of credit analysis.

6.	Evaluate the accuracy and integrity of the internal risk rating processes. Consider:

- Findings from the loan sample.

- The role of loan review.

7. Assess the process to ensure compliance with applicable laws, rulings, regulations, and accounting guidelines.

8. Evaluate the effectiveness of processes used to monitor collateral. Consider:

   - How duplicate invoices are reviewed for accuracy.
     - Are they reviewed for eligibility under the borrowing base definitions?
     - Are they monitored for customer credit quality?
     - Are they removed from the borrowing base as soon as delinquency exceeds eligibility limits on past-due items?
   - How borrowing base certifications are reviewed for accuracy.
     - Are agings received in a timely manner?
     - Are receivable listings reviewed for compliance with eligibility?
     - Are receivable listings periodically audited ?
     - Are over-advances immediately identified, including those created when delinquent receivables are eliminated?
   - How receivables collateral held against a blanket lien are monitored.
     - Are frequent (at least quarterly) financial statements received and promptly reviewed for adequacy of collateral?
     - Are audited financial statements required?
     - If audited statements are not required, is collateral somehow verified periodically?
   - How inventory is monitored.
     - Is the basis for valuation reasonable?
     - Does a system ensure that stale or obsolete inventory is removed from the borrowing base?
     - Is inventory periodically audited or subject to outside audit verification?
   - Whether the bank has a process to verify the perfection of liens.
   - Whether proper control is maintained over cash and collateral proceeds.

9. The examiner reviewing the ARIF portfolio should review the LPM examiner's findings to determine whether additional analysis is required for issues pertaining to:

   - Problem credit administration
   - Collections
   - Charge-offs

10. Review the method of evaluating, documenting, and maintaining the allowance for loan and lease losses. Determine whether the method is consistent with historical experience and current trends.

11. Verify the integrity of loan documentation. Assess the quality controls that ensure that credit documentation is complete.

12. Assess the risk limits management has established, evaluating both portfolio-wide limits and less comprehensive ones. After determining how much earnings or capital must be at risk before further analysis is triggered, decide whether these amounts are appropriate. Evaluate the plans management has developed to respond to breaches in defined risk tolerance levels.

13. Determine whether there are processes to monitor strategic and business plans for the portfolio. Consider the impact on earnings and capital as ARIF plans and strategies are executed.

14. Verify that the bank has an effective process to periodically evaluate internal controls. **(Note: The lack of an effective process may require examiners to conduct additional testing.)**

15. Evaluate the adequacy of internal controls within the ARIF unit. When considering segregation of duties, determine whether:

   - Delinquent account collection requests and past due notices are checked to the trial balances that are used to reconcile ARIF loan subsidiary records with general ledger accounts, and determine whether they are handled only by persons who do not also handle cash.
   - The preparation and posting of interest records is performed or reviewed by persons who do not also handle cash or issue official checks or drafts singly.
   - The employees responsible for receiving and releasing collateral to borrowers are not those responsible for making entries in the collateral register.
   - Someone not connected with loan processing handles collection notices.
   - Negotiable collateral is held under joint custody.

Personnel

Objective: To determine whether management and affected personnel display acceptable knowledge and technical skills to manage and perform their duties related to AR.

1. Determine whether the level of expertise and number of assigned personnel on the ARIF staff is adequate. Consider:

   - Whether staffing levels will support current operations or any planned growth.
   - Staff turnover.
   - The staff's previous ARIF and workout experience.
   - Specialized training provided.
   - The average account load per lending officer. Consider whether the load is reasonable in light of the complexity and condition of each officer's portfolio.
   - How senior management and the board of directors periodically evaluate the ARIF unit's understanding of and conformance with the bank's stated credit culture and loan policy. If there is no evaluation, determine the impact on the management of credit risk.

2. Assess the performance management and compensation programs for ARIF personnel. Consider whether these programs measure and reward behaviors that support the portfolio's strategic objectives and risk tolerance limits.

Controls

Objective: To determine the adequacy of loan review, internal/external audit, management information systems, internal controls, and any other control systems for ARIF.

1. Assess the effectiveness and independence of formal control functions. Control functions should have clear reporting lines, adequate resources, and the authority necessary to initiate change. Evaluate reporting lines to determine whether lenders could bring to bear undue influence on operations or control staff.

2. Determine the effectiveness of the loan review system in identifying risk in ARIF. Consider the following:

- Scope of loan review.
- Frequency of loan reviews.
- The number and qualifications of loan review personnel.
- Results of examination.
- Loan review's access to information and the board.
- Training opportunities or programs offered to loan review staff.
- Content of loan review reports, which should address:
  - The overall asset quality of the portfolio.
  - Trends in asset quality.
  - The quality of "significant" relationships.
  - The level and trend of policy, underwriting, and pricing exceptions.
  - Administrative, personnel, and underwriting issues.

3. Review the most recent loan review report for ARIF. Determine whether management has appropriately addressed weaknesses and areas of unwarranted risk.

4. Assess loan review's ability to identify problems as they develop. Determine whether problems have to be pronounced before loan review brings them to senior management's attention.

5. Determine whether management information systems provide timely, useful information to evaluate risk levels and trends in the ARIF portfolio.

6. Determine the adequacy of internal audit functions for ARIF. Consider:

- The scope of internal audit and results of the previous audit.
- Frequency of audits.
- The number and qualifications of internal audit personnel.
- Audit's access to information and the board.

7. Obtain from the examiner assigned internal and external audits a list of deficiencies noted in internal and external auditors' latest reviews. Determine whether management has appropriately addressed these deficiencies.

8. Evaluate the use of field audits, including their scope, timing, and frequency. Reports should include:

- Analysis of trends in turnover of receivables, inventory, and payables.

- Analysis of trends in sales, including returns, allowances, and discounts. Determine whether selected credit memos are tested.
- Testing of financial accounting records and controls.
- Verification of collateral.
- Assessment of overall transaction risk.
- Identification of potential compliance risk issues.

9. Evaluate the lender's response to deficiencies noted in field audits, including whether these responses are appropriate and timely relative to the risks identified.

10. Determine whether management's response to any material findings by any control group (including audit, loan review, and field audit units) has been verified and reviewed for objectivity and adequacy by senior management and the board (or a committee thereof).

Conclusions

Objective: To determine overall conclusions and communicate examination findings regarding the quantity of risk and management's ability to identify, measure, monitor and control risk in ARIF. To obtain commitments from management to initiate appropriate corrective action, if necessary.

1. Prepare a summary memorandum to the LPM examiner or EIC regarding the ARIF portfolio. Draft conclusions on:

    *   Asset quality of the portfolio.
    *   The adequacy of policies and underwriting standards.
    *   Volume and severity of underwriting and policy exceptions.
    *   Underwriting quality of sample loans.
    *   Quality of portfolio supervision.
    *   Concentrations of credit.
    *   Adequacy and timeliness of MIS.
    *   Adequacy of loan control functions.
    *   Compliance with applicable laws, rules, and regulations.
    *   Quality of staffing.
    *   Reliability of internal risk ratings.
    *   Appropriateness of strategic and business plans.
    *   The extent to which ARIF credit risk and credit risk management practices affect aggregate loan portfolio risk.
    *   Recommended corrective action regarding deficient policies, procedures, and practices. (Include whether management commits to the corrective action.)
    *   Any other concerns.

2. Provide input to help the EIC assign the bank CAMELS component ratings for asset quality and management.

3. Recommend risk assessments for the ARIF portfolio. Refer to the "Large Bank Supervision" and "Community Bank Supervision" booklets in the *Comptroller's Handbook* for guidance.

4. Based on discussions with the EIC, bank management, and information in the summary memorandum, prepare a brief comment on ARIF for inclusion in the ROE.

5.   Discuss examination findings and conclusions with the examiner
      assigned loan portfolio management and the EIC. If necessary, compose
      "Matters Requiring Board Attention" (MRBA) for the loan portfolio
      management examination. MRBAs should cover practices that:

      •   Deviate from sound, fundamental principles and are likely to result
          in financial deterioration if not addressed, or
      •   Result in substantive noncompliance with laws.

      MRBAs should discuss:

      •   Causes of the problem.
      •   Consequences of inaction.
      •   Management's commitment to corrective action.
      •   The time frame and persons responsible for corrective action.

6.   Discuss findings with bank management, including conclusions about
      risks. Obtain commitments for corrective action.

7.   Write a memorandum specifically setting out what the OCC should do in
      the future to effectively supervise the ARIF at this bank. Include time
      frames, staffing, and workdays required.

8.   Update the supervisory record and any applicable report of examination
      schedules or tables.

9.   Update the examination work papers in accordance with OCC guidance.

ARIF Summary Chart

The following chart summarizes the features of the three types of ARIF discussed in this booklet.

	Asset-Based Lending	Secured Financing	Blanket Receivables Lending
Borrowing Base	Yes. ARIF updated daily or weekly. Borrowing base certifications weekly or monthly.	Yes. ARIF updated monthly. Borrowing base certifications monthly or quarterly.	No. Advance rates used for valuing collateral or informal guidance.
Loan Disbursements	Funds advanced by bank against specific invoices or trade documents.	Borrower draws against borrowing base availability.	Borrower draws against note availability.
Cash Receipts	Payments are made directly to a bank-controlled lock box and applied to the loan balance.	Payments are made to the borrower, and the borrower makes discretionary loan payments.	Payments are made to the borrower, and the borrower makes discretionary loan payments.
Field Audits	Yes. Frequency ranges from weekly to quarterly based on risk.	Yes. Annually.	No.
Appraisals (Inventory)	Yes.	Yes for higher risk credits. Otherwise, may rely on field audit.	Generally only in a liquidation.
Financial Statements	Quarterly certified. Monthly management.	Annual certified. Quarterly management.	Annual certified or reviewed.
Financial Covenants	Yes. Quarterly compliance.	Yes. Quarterly compliance.	Varies.

Accounts Receivable and Inventory Financing

Trade Cycle Analysis Worksheet

Rules of Thumb

- Should be performed at the low point of the operating cycle.
- Needs to be a seasonal operating cycle.
- Credit expects to repay at the end of the operating cycle (does not apply to floor-plan lines or asset-based loans that involve ongoing borrowings).
- Does not apply to companies with more than one operating cycle (e.g., companies having several product lines with different seasonality).

How to Calculate Trade Cycle Components

TRADE CYCLE ANALYSIS	DAYS SALES
ARF ÷ SPD	
+ Inventory ÷ SPD	
= Operating Cycle	
- AP ÷ SPD	
- Accruals ÷ SPD	
- Working Capital ÷ SPD	
= Net Days *	
Net Days (If Positive)	
X SPD	
= Additional Working Capital	

SPD = Sales Per Day {$ Sales ÷ 360 Days}

* If net days are negative, the borrower has sufficient permanent working capital to clean up seasonal borrowings. If net days are positive, the borrower lacks sufficient permanent working capital to clean up seasonal borrowings. To determine the amount of additional working capital needed to support the operating cycle, multiply net days times sales per day. The product is the approximate working capital shortfall.

ADVERSE RISK RATING EXAMPLES

EXAMPLE A

Borrower: Motoparts Manufacturing Co., Inc.
Carsville, USA

Business: Manufacturer of specialized components for the
automobile industry.

Facility $5MM RC with a decreasing term sub-limit on
Description: machinery, equipment, and real estate. Originated four
years ago at $4MM. Increased to current amount two years
ago. Matures in three months.   Interest is current.

Pricing: Prime + 150 basis points. RC is interest only.

Repayment: Term portion amortizes monthly over seven years.
Reductions in term loan add to availability back to the RC.

Repayment   RC through conversion of current assets to cash. Term
Sources: portion through operating CF and conversion of current
assets to cash.

Collateral: Eligible accounts receivable and inventory, at 87.5% and
65% advance rates respectively. $4.3MM outstanding
under RC, leaving $200M available under borrowing base
formula. M & E valued at $2.7MM and RE at $120M.
Term outstanding is $500M.

Financial Synopsis:

- Financial condition is characterized by ongoing
  operating losses, significant deficit working capital, and
  deficit tangible net worth.
- Weakened liquidity has resulted in extensive line
  reliance, with borrower frequently near maximum
  borrowing availability even after increase in advance

rates on accounts receivable and inventory from 80% and 60% to current levels.

- Virtually all assets are pledged to secure debts.
- Projected increased funding needs for CAPEX, WC, and debt service.
- $4MM borrowing outside this debt matures in 10 months and failure to refinance could trigger bankruptcy.

Current Status: One of two manufacturing divisions is profitable, but drag from the other division precludes return to company-wide positive earnings. Management is addressing problems at the weaker division; however, realization of a turnaround has been slower than anticipated.

Risk Rating Decision:
Substandard/Accrual

- Weak financial position, characterized by deficit working capital and deficit tangible net worth.
- Continuing losses.
- High leverage.
- Thin collateral coverage.
- Strong potential for refinancing problems and bankruptcy.
- Inability to meet plan to stem losses in weaker of two divisions.

Risk Rating Considerations:

- Adequate controls are not sufficient to overcome high risk of default.
- Need to increase advance rates for more than a short-term seasonal need are indicative of well-defined weakness in the credit.

Alternate scenario:

- Cash flow analysis reveals interest and term debt principal reductions being made from RC draws.
- Debt outside this loan matures in less than two months and company has been unable to arrange refinance.

Risk Rating - Alternate scenario:

- Remains substandard.
- Nonaccrual.

Risk Rating Discussion - Alternate scenario:

- Either CF weakness or inability to arrange refinance would trigger placing debt on nonaccrual status.

EXAMPLE B

Borrower: Tschockies International, Inc.
Tackytown, USA

Business: Home decoration and crafts distribution.

Facility Description: $3.5MM one-year revolver with annual renewal. Line originated three years ago and has never achieved off-season payout, as projected at inception. Currently fully advanced. Line is governed by borrowing base of accounts receivable and inventory. Reporting includes monthly borrowing base certificates and accounts receivable aging. Terms also provide for periodic field audits. The last audit was performed 21 months ago. Loan has been governed by forbearance agreement for five months; bank is implementing an exit strategy and has increased pricing.

Pricing: Bank floating base + 200 basis points.

Repayment Sources: Primary: Conversion of current assets to cash.
Secondary: Refinance of debt or sale of business.

Guaranty: None.

Covenants: Covenants are measured and enforced annually at quarter-end:

Covenant	Required Level	Actual	Interim 5 mos.
Minimum EBIT/Interest	1.4x	0.98x	0.94x
Maximum Debt/NW	8.0x	8.70x	8.74x
Minimum Fixed Charge Coverage[1]	1.0x	0.91x	0.89x

[1] Defined as EBITDA-CAPEX • Debt service.

The company triggered covenant defaults in each of the past two quarters. The first covenant defaults were waived for a fee, with no modifications to structure or terms. After the second default, the bank served notice of default, implemented penalty pricing, and initiated an exit strategy.

Collateral: Borrowing base totals $3.5MM. It consists of eligible ARs of $1.4MM, with an 80% advance rate, providing $1.1MM in availability and eligible inventory of $3.4MM, with a 70% advance rate, providing $2.4MM availability. Only ineligible ARs are those greater than 90 days past due.

Financial Synopsis:

- Problems with installation of inventory software system weakened controls and impaired the firm's ability to fill orders. Additionally, 75% of inventory (which provides most availability) could not be accounted for, and the borrower's customers located other sources of merchandise.

- Fiscal year-end sales revenues declined 22% and CF has dropped dramatically because of the sales decline and the lack of liquidity in current assets. Operating losses have been recorded for two years.

- Infusion of cash, in the form of subordinated debt assumed by principals, averted default. Principals have declared an inability to make future cash infusions.

Current Status: Physical inventory by audit firm is almost complete; preliminary results indicate that inventory write downs will be required. Satisfactory inventory results are needed to support a refinancing package that will retire this debt.

Risk Rating Decision:
Substandard/Nonaccrual
- Operating losses and negative CF.
- High leverage.
- Impaired liquidity position.
- Inadequate or tight collateral coverage at best.

Risk Rating Considerations:
- Although takeout financing has been arranged (but not finalized), the current condition of the borrower warrants classification.
- Credit possesses well-defined weakness, insufficient DSC, and operating losses.
- No basis for accrual status. Given the questions surrounding collateral values, accrual status is not supported. Significant write-

downs in inventory indicate the credit is not well secured and will jeopardize the takeout financing package.

EXAMPLE C

Borrower: Jack's Sprouts, Inc.
Beantown, USA

Business: Seed processing and distribution.

Facility Description: $3.3 MM three-year revolver. Line originated 6-01 at $3MM amended to $3.3MM from 4-02 to 6-02, and matures 6-03. Inventory sublimit of $2.1MM. Current outstandings are $3.1MM. Line is fully followed with weekly borrowing base certificates and accounts receivable agings. Terms also provide for periodic field audits.

Pricing: LIBOR + 300 basis points

Repayment Sources: Primary: Conversion of current assets to cash. Secondary: Refinance or sale of company. Tertiary: Liquidation of assets.

Guaranty: Owner guarantees, but financial statement indicates only nominal support from that source.

Covenants: Covenants are measured quarterly.

Covenant	Required Level	FYE-01	Interim (9 mo.) 3Q'02
Minimum EBIT/Interest	1.10x	1.12x	1.15x
Maximum Debt/TNW	4.0x	1.45x	3.40x
Minimum Fixed Charge Coverage[1]	1.05x	1.10x	.99x

[1] Defined as EBITDA-CAPEX ÷ Debt service

The company violated the leverage coverage during FY-01; the bank reset the covenants with no further modifications.

Collateral: Eligible accounts receivable of $1,940M, based on an 80% advance rate. Eligible inventory of $2,520M, based on a

50% advance rate. Only ARs considered ineligible are those more than 90 days past due.

Financial Synopsis:

- Company has experienced interim operating losses and negative cash flow caused primarily by high selling expenses, general expenses, and administrative expenses following a recent acquisition.
- Company did not meet projections for FY-01 because of higher-than-planned GSA and a modest shortfall in revenue.
- Liquidity has declined with current ratio of 1.16 on 3-02 interim compared with 1.31 at FYE-01.

Current Status: Interest is current. Line availability is tight. Line was over-advanced during 1Q'02, but over-advance was cleared prior to end of 1Q'02 when the company moved into its strong spring selling season. Most recent field exam 2-02 (four mos. ago) reported satisfactory results. Nine-month performance through 2Q'02 shows some improvement, but remains behind budget.

Risk Rating Decision:

Special Mention/Accrual

- Adequate interest coverage.
- Weak operating performance.
- Tight liquidity.
- Moderately high leverage.
- Unplanned, seasonal over-advance, subsequently cleared.
- Good controls over high quality accounts receivable and inventory.

Risk Rating Considerations:

- Controls and collateral quality are satisfactory.
- This is a classic example of a company that meets the SM criteria of "potential weaknesses that deserve management's close attention and may result in deterioration of the repayment prospects for the asset or in the institution's credit position at some future date."
- Concern is highlighted by the inability to meet plans and continuing weak operating performance.

Alternate scenario:

- New field audit discovers that 50% of the inventory consists of out-of-date seeds.

- The borrowing base is adjusted resulting in a $350M over-advance. Inventory write-downs produce a sizable loss for FYE-02

- Leverage increases to 5X and interest coverage drops to 1.05x. Company indicates sales in FY-03 will decline unless they receive additional financing to acquire new inventory.

- Company is working with consultants to develop a new business plan. Sale of the company is a possibility. Owner feels the business is worth $5MM. Other than leases on some equipment and a real estate mortgage, there is no other financing.

Risk Rating - Alternate scenario:
Substandard/Accrual

- Interest coverage has tightened, but remains adequate.
- Substantial net loss and questionable ability to restore operations.
- Tight liquidity.
- High leverage.
- Over-advance.
- Collateral shortfall.

Risk Rating Discussion - Alternate scenario:

- The accrual decision and rating will have to be re-evaluated when the business plan is submitted.

- Adequate interest coverage and the probability that additional collateral is available to cover the shortfall preclude nonaccrual status.

- If the business plan does not support a reasonable turn-around strategy and the over-advance is not collateralized, the loan should be placed on nonaccrual and a split substandard/doubtful or loss rating may be appropriate.

Accounts Payable - A current liability representing the amount owed by an individual or a business to a creditor for merchandise or services purchased on open account or short-term credit.

Accounts Receivable - Money owed a business for merchandise or services bought on open account. Accounts receivable arise from the business practice of providing a customer merchandise or a service with the expectation of receiving payment per specified terms. The terms are included on the seller's invoice to the buyer with no written evidence of debt executed between seller and buyer.

Advance - A drawdown or disbursement of funds according to the terms of an existing loan agreement. Advances are common to revolving credit facilities. The term can also refer to a customer paying its accounts payable prior to the agreed-upon date.

Advance Rate - The maximum percentage that the lender will lend against a type of collateral. The advance rate will vary by the type of collateral, terms, age, and perhaps the financial strength of the obligated party.

Aging (Schedule) - A periodic report listing a borrower's accounts receivable or payable balances, by customer or supplier, detailing the current status or delinquency of the balances owed or owing. The report is usually used in determining the borrower's compliance with the borrowing base requirements in the loan agreement.

Asset-Based Lending (ABL) - A specialized form of secured lending whereby a company uses its current assets (accounts receivable and inventory) as collateral for a loan. The loan is structured so that the amount of credit is limited in relation to the value of the collateral. The product is differentiated from other types of lending secured by accounts receivable and inventory by the lender's use of controls over the borrower's cash receipts and disbursements and the quality of collateral.

Availability - The additional funds that the lender will advance under the terms of the credit facility. The amount is often the difference between the loan commitment amount and the outstanding balance of the credit facility. In most cases, the terms of the credit agreement limit the amount available if the commitment amount is greater than the borrowing base.

Blanket Assignment - An agreement giving the lender a security interest in all of assets owned by the borrower. As used by some lenders, the term is meant as a catch-all security interest covering every anticipated type of asset owned by the borrower. To perfect the lender's security interest in the borrower's personal property, the lender must file a financing statement describing the collateral in all its locations. To perfect the lender's security interest in all real or titled property, the lender must specify the assets in the appropriate documents and must file the documents in the proper jurisdiction. If the assets are already encumbered and the borrower has limited equity in them, the lender may not expend the resources to perfect its security interest in the borrower's real and titled property.

Borrowing Base - A collateral base, agreed to by the borrower and lender, which is used to limit the amount of funds the lender will advance the borrower. The borrowing base specifies the maximum amount that can be borrowed in terms of collateral type, eligibility, and advance rates.

Compliance Certifications - The borrower's statement certifying its adherence to the terms of the loan agreement during the stated period. The certificate is usually completed by the company's principal financial officer. If the borrower is in compliance with the terms of loan agreement (no event of default has occurred), the principal financial officer will attest accordingly. Supporting data is usually required to document the assertion.

Consignment - The physical transfer of goods from a seller or vendor to another legal entity that acts as a selling agent for the seller. The seller is known as the "consignor" or the goods, and title to the goods remains with the seller. The receiver of the goods under consignment is known as the "consignee." The consignee acts as agent for the consignor, sells the goods for a commission, and remits the net proceeds to the consignor. The consignor does not recognize revenue until the consignee sells the goods to a third party.

Contra-Accounts - They arise when a borrower has both accounts receivable and accounts payable with the same entity because the party is both a customer and a supplier of the borrower. These accounts are usually considered ineligible collateral.

Credit Memo - A detailed memorandum forwarded from one party or firm to another granting credit for returned merchandise, some omission, overpayment, or other cause. It may also refer to the posting medium authorizing the credit to a specific account, including details of the transaction and signature or initials of the party authorizing the credit.

Cross-Aging - The practice of making all of the accounts receivable from a single account party (the obligated party for an account receivable) ineligible to be included in the borrowing base if a specified proportion of the total accounts receivable from that party is delinquent. Also, sometimes referred to as the "10 percent rule" since a common delinquency threshold is 10 percent.

Cross-Collateralized - In the event of default, the collateral of cross-collateralized loans is used to satisfy the debts. In most instances the collateral is shared on a pari passu basis. The terms of the agreement can also specify that only the excess collateral of one loan can be shifted to satisfy another.

Cross Default - The right to declare a loan in default if an event of default occurs in another loan.

Debtor-in-Possession (DIP) Financing - Financing provided to a borrower after a chapter 11 (reorganization) bankruptcy filing. A lender provides the DIP post-petition financing to support its working capital needs while the DIP attempts to rehabilitate its financial condition and emerge from bankruptcy protection. In order to encourage lenders to provide DIP financing, the bankruptcy code grants the DIP lender a priority claim on the DIP's assets. This provides the DIP lender protection in the event the DIP fails to emerge from chapter 11 and liquidates. Liquidation can be accomplished either in chapter 11 or by converting the case to a chapter 7 filing.

Desk Following (Desk-Followed) - A term used to describe less rigorous, informal monitoring of an ARIF loan. Desk following is usually found only in blanket receivables lending and some secured financing.

Eligible Collateral - A defined term in the loan agreement that controls what collateral can be included in the borrowing base.

Factoring - An arrangement in which a company shortens its cash cycle by selling its accounts receivable without recourse to a third party, known as a "factor." A factor assumes the full risk of collection, including credit losses. There are two basic types of factoring: (1) discount factoring, in which the factor discounts the receivables prior to the maturity date, and (2) maturity factoring, in which the factor pays the client the purchase price of the factored accounts at maturity. Factors frequently perform all accounting functions in connection with the accounts receivable, in which case purchasers are notified to remit payments directly to the factor.

Formula - A calculation to determine the borrowing base in which a margin or advance rate is applied to each type of collateral.

Full Following - A term describing the process ABL lenders use to closely control credit availability and collateral by means of a borrowing base, control of the cash receipts, and field audits.

Ineligible Collateral - Pledged receivables or inventory that does not meet the criteria specified in the loan agreement. Ineligible collateral remains part of the ABL lender's collateral pool, but does not qualify for inclusion in the borrowing base.

Lien - A legal right granted by the authority of a court to control or to enforce a charge against another's property until some legal claim is paid or otherwise satisfied.

Liquidation Value - The most likely price an asset will bring if it is sold without reasonable market exposure and when the seller is under duress. Sometimes the liquidation value is based on an orderly liquidation that allows for a brief marketing period as contrasted with a forced liquidation value that is based on an auction sale.

Lock Box - A cash management product offered by financial institutions that accelerates a client's collection of receivables. The client's customers are directed to make payments to regionally located post office boxes, where they are picked up several times each day and entered into an automated check processing system. By processing checks by region, the client gains faster access to its funds since it speeds their presentment to the bank they are drawn on. Lenders use lock boxes in ABL financing to control cash receipts.

Margin - The difference between the market value of collateral pledged to secure a loan and the amount the bank will advance against the collateral.

Market Value - The most likely price an asset will bring if it is sold in a competitive, open market, with reasonable market exposure and willing, informed buyers and sellers.

Non-notification - The bank does not notify the borrower's pledged accounts that they are to remit payments directly to the bank. Non-notification often involves a lock box arrangement. The bank may also allow the borrower to collect payments and remit them to the bank for credit against the loan balance.

Notification - The bank notifies a borrower's pledged accounts that they are to remit payments directly to the bank for collection.

Operating Cycle - The period of time it takes a business to convert purchased and manufactured goods and services into sales, plus the time to collect the cash from the associated sales. If the company has sold receivables through factoring arrangements, the calculation will be distorted.

Pari Passu - Credit facilities in which two or more lenders are accorded equal treatment under a loan agreement. Most frequently applied to collateral, but may also refer to loan structure, documentation, maturity, or any other substantive condition

Purchase Money Security Interest (PMSI) - The Uniform Commercial Code (UCC) prescribes that if a creditor provides financing for a debtor to acquire specific goods, the creditor can perfect a security interest in the goods despite the existence of financing statements on similarly described collateral. However, the creditor must adhere to strict rules to perfect a PMSI. If the creditor violates the PMSI requirements, the creditor's lien will be junior to the previously perfected financing statements.

Revolving Credit Facility - A loan agreement that allows the borrower to frequently draw down and repay advances. The proceeds are usually used to support the working capital needs of the borrower. A borrowing base requirement in the loan agreement commonly mitigates the lender's credit risk.

Security Agreement - A document giving a lender a security interest in assets pledged as collateral. This agreement, signed by the borrower, describes the collateral and its location in sufficient detail so the lender can identify it, and assigns to the lender the right to sell or dispose of the assigned collateral if the borrower is unable to pay the obligation.

Set-off (offset) - A common law right of a lender to seize deposits owned by a debtor and deposited in the lender's institution for nonpayment of an obligation. It also occurs in settlement of mutual debt between a debtor in bankruptcy and a creditor, through offsetting claims. Instead of receiving cash payment, debtors credit the amount owed against the other party's obligations to them. This allows creditors to collect more than they otherwise would have collected under a debt repayment plan approved by a bankruptcy court.

Trade Cycle Analysis - A method of computing whether working capital is sufficient to support the working investment need of a business. (See "operating cycle.")

Uniform Commercial Code (UCC) - A model framework of laws that addresses commercial transactions. Each state may modify or exclude provisions of the model framework when adopting the UCC. While the UCC varies from state to state, the spirit of the state-adopted statutes is basically consistent. The UCC was set forth to stimulate interstate commerce by providing a fair measure of consistency among states' commercial laws.

Weighted Average Risk Rating - Statistical measure of the total risk in a portfolio of loans. The weighted average risk rating (WARR) is calculated by multiplying the loan commitment amount (or outstandings) by the risk rating for each loan in the portfolio, aggregating, and dividing by the total portfolio commitment (or outstandings).

Working Investment - The result of calculating the sum of accounts receivable and inventory, minus the sum of accounts payable and accrued expenses (excluding taxes). It represents the amount of financing and trade support that a company needs to fund its trading assets.

Accounts Receivable and Inventory Financing

References

Laws

General Powers (Seventh)	12 USC 24
Lending Limits	12 USC 84
Loans to Affiliates	12 USC 371c
Loans to Insiders	12 USC 375a 12 USC 375b
Safety and Soundness (FIDICIA)	12 USC 1831p-1
Tie-in Provisions	12 USC 1972

Regulations

Lending Limits	12 CFR 32
Loans to Insiders	12 CFR 215
Purchase of Open Accounts	12 CFR 7.1020
Retention of Credit Files	12 CFR 103.33(a)
Safety and Soundness	12 CFR 30

www.ingramcontent.com/pod-product-compliance
Lightning Source LLC
Chambersburg PA
CBHW080518290526
45790CB00006B/2220